CULTURES OF THE WORLD™

MALAYSIA

Heidi Munan/Foo Yuk Yee

BENCHMARK BOOKS

MARSHALL CAVENDISH
NEW YORK

PICTURE CREDITS
APA, Bes Stock, Wendy Chan, Barbara Dare, Jane Duff,
Cathay Pacific, Foto Technik, HBL Network Photo
Agency, Jill Gocher, Image Bank, Peter Korn, Mako
Sub-aquatics, Malaysian Tourist Promotion Board, MAS,
Ministry of Information Malaysia, Heidi Munan,
National Archives of Malaysia, Orang Asli Museum,
Photobank, Radio Television Malaysia, Michael Spilling,
Tourist Development Corporation of Malaysia

ACKNOWLEDGMENTS
With special thanks to Foon Yew Secondary School,
Johor Bahru, and Majlis Ugama Islam Singapura

PRECEDING PAGE:
Malaysian schoolgirls wave their country flag at the
National Day parade.

Marshall Cavendish Corporation
99 White Plains Road
Tarrytown, NY 10591
Website: www.marshallcavendish.com

Originated and designed by
Times Books International, an imprint of
Times Media Private Limited, a member of the
Times International Publishing Group

Printed in Malaysia

Library of Congress Cataloging-in-Publication Data:
Munan, Heidi.
   Malaysia / Heidi Munan.
      p. cm. — (Cultures of the world)
   Includes bibliographical references and index.
   ISBN 0-7614-1351-0
   1. Malaysia—Juvenile literature. [1. Malaysia.] I. Title.
II. Series.

DS592. M85 2001
959.5—dc21   2001025302

6 5 4 3

CONTENTS

An Iban wearing a headdress. The Iban are one of the main tribes in East Malaysia.

Getting used to holiday gear. Malay children wear traditional clothing during Malay festivals.

INTRODUCTION

LOCATED IN SOUTHEAST ASIA, Malaysia lies just north of the equator. The country consists of two parts: East Malaysia (Sabah and Sarawak) and West, or Peninsular, Malaysia. Thailand lies to the north of Peninsular Malaysia, while the island state of Singapore lies at its southern tip. The South China Sea separates Peninsular Malaysia from East Malaysia, which is located on the Indonesian island of Borneo.

Malaysia is endowed with natural resources. It has large reserves of petroleum and natural gas and is a leading exporter of tin, rubber, palm oil, and tropical hardwoods. With luxuriant rainforests, the country is also rich in plant and animal life.

Malaysia's wealth of natural treasures is matched by its ethnic diversity. The government encourages intermingling among the three major ethnic groups—Malay, Chinese, and Indian. Racial and religious harmony in the country has created an eclectic mixture of cultures. As a result, Malaysians enjoy a wide range of festivals and cuisines.

GEOGRAPHY

THE TWO PARTS OF MALAYSIA make up a total land area of 127,284 square miles (329,750 square km), slightly larger than New Mexico. Between East Malaysia (consisting of the states of Sabah and Sarawak) and West Malaysia (known as Peninsular Malaysia) lie about 330 miles (531 km) of the South China Sea.

Both parts of Malaysia lie in the equatorial rainfall zone, just north of the equator. In the days of sailing ships, harbors along the Straits of Melaka and on the southern tip of the Malay Peninsula were used by traders during the monsoon season as safe ports in which to weather the storms in the South China Sea.

SEASONS

Malaysia has two seasons—wet and very wet. Rain falls daily during the monsoon season (October to April), but even during the drier part of the year, there are a couple of showers a week. Kuala Lumpur records an average of 198 rainy days a year and Kota Kinabalu 179. But Kuching holds the record with 246 rainy days a year! Year round the average humidity at around 2 P.M. ranges from 60 to 73 percent. Temperatures in Malaysia range from 77°F (25°C) to 95°F (35°C), with mostly cool nights. "Cool" means that in hilly areas it is advisable to sleep under a light blanket. A cotton sheet suffices for sleepers in the low-lying areas.

Above: **This longhouse in Sarawak has a great view of a lake in the foreground and forested mountains behind.**

Opposite: **Malaysia's coastlines boast sunshine, white sands, and swaying palms.**

7

PENINSULAR MALAYSIA

The 11 states of Peninsular Malaysia extend from the state of Johor at the southern tip of the peninsula (separated from Singapore by the Straits of Johor) to the Thai border in the north. These states include several offshore islands.

The peninsula's backbone of mountains, Banjaran Titiwangsa, runs from north to south with short rivers draining into either the Straits of Melaka to the west or the South China Sea to the east. The mountain range rises to over 6,500 feet (1,981 m) in places and is a serious obstacle to east–west traffic. A road from Kuala Lumpur in the west to Kuantan in the east was completed in 1911 and another to Kota Bharu in 1982. In 1988 the North–South highway was completed, connecting western Peninsular Malaysia from Johor to Kuala Lumpur.

All the 11 states have access to the sea, from the 307 square miles (795 square km) of tiny Perlis Indera Kayangan, tucked away between Kedah Darul Aman and Thailand, to the 13,886 square miles (35,965 square km) of majestic Pahang Darulmakmur in the center of the peninsula. Kedah is a land of fertile plains devoted to rice growing, while huge estates of oil palm, cocoa, and rubber are found in the lowlands of Johor.

The states of Kelantan and Terengganu are east of the main mountain range. Undulating plains lie open to the South China Sea, which traditionally provides a living for the fearless fishermen living in these states. Perak, Selangor, and Negeri Sembilan occupy the western coast south of Kedah. Tin ore is found in these three states, which gave them corresponding political and economic importance in the 19th century. Melaka (or Malacca) was a major trading port until the arrival of the Portuguese in 1511. Pulau Pinang (Penang Island) rose to prominence as a port in the late 18th century.

Above: **Kedah's fertile rice fields.**

Opposite: **A view of the island of Penang with the mainland in the background.**

SABAH AND SARAWAK

East Malaysia lies on the island of Borneo, north of the Indonesian province of Kalimantan. The two East Malaysian states, Sarawak and Sabah, share many physical characteristics. Until recent times, rivers were the most common transportation routes in both states, and the main settlements were within the tidal estuaries. Early exports included jungle produce, birds' nests, and other rarities.

Sabah occupies 28,460 square miles (73,711 square km) of Borneo's northeastern corner. Its profile is dominated by the Crocker Range (where Mt. Kinabalu stands), which extends toward the south, forming the watershed between Sarawak and Kalimantan. Sabah's main rivers drain into the Sulu Sea, where Sandakan, the territory's first capital, is situated.

Above: **Sarawak's main rivers, the Rajang and the Baram, rise in the highlands along the state's eastern fringe.**

Right: **An aerial view of Sabah.**

Today's capital, Kota Kinabalu, is located on Sabah's western coast.

Of Sarawak's total land area of 48,050 square miles (124,449 square km), only about one-fifth is suitable for agriculture. Wide tracts of mangrove swamps or semi-saline swamp forest on the coast are sources of many natural products but are otherwise agriculturally unproductive. The capital, Kuching, is located in Sarawak's western corner.

Kuala Lumpur combines modern skyscrapers (left) and superhighways with remnants of its early days of independence (below).

KUALA LUMPUR

Kuala Lumpur, the capital of Malaysia, began as a Chinese tin mining settlement belonging to the Sultan of Selangor. The original township stood where the Gombak and Kelang rivers merged to form a delta. Hence the name Kuala Lumpur: *kuala* describes a delta, a feature that forms where rivers meet or flow into the sea; *lumpur* means "muddy."

Present-day Kuala Lumpur is a modern city equipped with a generally efficient infrastructure, large shopping complexes, and first-class hotels. Radio taxis and mini- and omnibuses serve the transportation needs of locals and tourists alike. But drainage is still a problem in low-lying areas. Traffic comes to a standstill when heavy monsoon rains cause flash floods.

Kuala Lumpur is a Federal Territory administered separately from its parent state, Selangor. Centrally located on the western coast of the Malay Peninsula, Kuala Lumpur is the center of the Malaysian federal government. The national university, the national mosque, and the head offices of most big businesses are also located here.

Like many Southeast Asian cities, Kuala Lumpur attracts an influx of migrants from rural areas. Unable to find ready and affordable housing, these people are forced to live in congested urban squatter villages.

The sandy beaches of Batu Ferringhi along the northern shore of Penang attract avid sunseekers year-round.

PENANG

Pulau Pinang (Penang Island), founded by Captain Francis Light of the British East India Company in the 18th century, was an important trading station in the Malay Peninsula until the 19th century. It declined in importance when Singapore, off the southern tip of the peninsula, rose to prominence in the 1820s.

Penang had a good natural harbor where ship captains could wait out the fierce monsoons, do a little quiet trading in Kedah, Perlis, Perak, or Sumatra, and then return to Calcutta in India after the winds had changed.

Penang's industries include rubber processing, textile manufacture, and food production. Tin from Perak and southern Thailand is smelted in Penang, and Thai rice is imported in bulk and redistributed throughout Malaysia from Penang. However Penang's economy still relies heavily on commerce and tourism.

Ferries regularly ply between George Town on the island of Penang and the town of Butterworth on the mainland. A regular air service also links Penang to the peninsula and the world.

The world's third-longest bridge now connects Penang to Province Wellesley on the mainland. The Malaysian prime minister opened the 8.4-mile (13.5-km) bridge in 1985 by driving across it in a Malaysia-made car, the Proton Saga.

TRANSPORTATION

River transportation, the traditional mode of transportation in Malaysia, remains important for some settlements in Sabah and Sarawak. This is because East Malaysia does not have as extensive a network of roads as Peninsular Malaysia, where river transportation has lost its importance except in parts of the eastern coast.

The peninsula has one of the best road systems in the region. There are four major highways: one lines the western coast from the Malaysian/Thai border to the southern tip of the peninsula; another links Port Kelang on the western coast to Kuantan on the eastern coast; a third runs from Kuantan north to Kota Bharu; and the fourth runs from Johor Bahru to Kuala Lumpur.

Malaysia's rail system is largely confined to the peninsula. It extends into Singapore in the south, while in the north, it connects with the State Railway of Thailand, thus enabling travel by rail to the two neighboring countries. An "Orient Express" running from Singapore to Bangkok was launched in 1993.

Rail transportation is also well developed on the peninsula. In East Malaysia, there is a rail line only between Kota Kinabalu and Tenom in Sabah. Coastal and sea transportation systems in Malaysia are important, given the country's long coastline. Coastal and river ports include George Town and Port Kelang in Peninsular Malaysia and Kuching, Sibu, Labuan, Kota Kinabalu, Sandakan, and Tawau in East Malaysia.

Air transportation is growing rapidly and is an important link between East and Peninsular Malaysia, with regular internal services between Kuala Lumpur, Kuching, and Kota Kinabalu. Also a fleet of small aircraft maintains vital links in the remote areas of East Malaysia. There are international airports in Johor Bahru, Kuala Lumpur, and Penang. The modern Kuala Lumpur International Airport was completed in 1998.

WILDLIFE

Malaysia's best-known national park is the Taman Negara in the state of Pahang. Set in 1,677 square miles (4,343 square km) of dense tropical forest surrounding the East Coast Range, the Taman Negara includes Gunung Tahan, the highest peak in Peninsular Malaysia at 7,174 feet (2,187 m).

The Taman Negara can be reached only by river. There are no roads leading directly into the park. Kuala Tembeling is the last terminus for travelers by road and rail. From there, visitors have to travel by boat to Kuala Tahan and the chalet-style lodgings at the foot of the mountain.

Flora and fauna are painstakingly preserved in the Taman Negara, making the park a paradise for birdwatchers, butterfly hunters (armed with a camera), simian fanciers, or adventure seekers who enjoy the thrill of getting close to a tiger or a wild buffalo—both rare but still found in this national park.

In Sarawak, the Bako National Park preserves a slice of coastal and lowland forests for future generations, and the Niah National Park protects spectacular limestone caves. No national park in Malaysia is easy to reach, and the 7,668-acre (3,103-hectare) Niah is no exception. A bumpy 112-mile (180-km) drive from Miri takes visitors to Batu Niah. From there it is a short boat ride to Pengkalan Lobang. Finally a 2.5-mile (4-km) walk through the park, partly on a plank, brings the visitors to the caves' western entrance.

Hides like this In the Taman Negara make it possible to observe jungle animals in safety. At 16 feet (5 m) above ground, viewers are out of the reach of elephants.

Above: **An orangutan at play.**

Below: **The wild, windswept summit of Mount Kinabalu, or Akin Nabalu, "home of the spirits of the departed."**

MOUNT KINABALU

At 13,455 feet (4,101 m), Mount Kinabalu is the highest peak in Southeast Asia. Rising within view of the sea, it actually seems to be "near as high as Mount Everest" as a startled World War II pilot described it when the huge mass suddenly appeared in front of his fragile craft.

Mount Kinabalu is the center of one of Malaysia's most popular national parks, the Kinabalu National Park in Sabah. The park's 306 square miles (793 square km) include lowland rainforest, hill forest, "cloud forest" (mossy vegetation shrouded in mist and moisture), subalpine grass patches, and bare, wind-scrubbed granite near the summit.

The Kinabalu National Park is a botanist's dream. The parasitic Rafflesia with its 3-foot (1-m) bloom is found here, as are many varieties of fungi, including the "sunburst," and fern trees 13 feet (4 m) high. Ground orchids, tree orchids, cliff orchids, and the tiny Podochilus just visible to the naked eye all grow wild in this park. The rainforest of the Kinabalu National Park teems with nepenthes, graceful pitcher plants that hold up to 7 pints of liquid and trap live insects in their depths.

Malaysia's wildlife is well represented in this park. Bats and squirrels, shrews and tarsiers, and the slow loris (which really does move slowly) make their home here. Monkeys and apes, including the friendly orangutan, thrive in this protected area. The pangolin is safe here from greedy gourmets, as are the deer, boars, and nearly 300 species of birds.

HISTORY

EARLY PEOPLES LEFT CLUES that tell us a lot about the way they lived and the things they did. Pot shards, worked stone and wood fragments, traces of villages and towns, and cave paintings are just some of the physical manifestations of early habitation. In Malaysia such precious materials are vulnerable to destruction in the warm and humid climate. The moisture-laden atmosphere speeds up the rate at which raw wood rots and metals rust, and creeping plants and mosses soon shroud stone structures. Thus Malaysia's prehistory has been pieced together from accidental discoveries of ancient objects in caves, burial sites, and ritual deposits in dry, gravelly soils. Nevertheless, what is known is fascinating.

Humans were living in the Niah Caves in Sarawak 40,000 years ago, as a skull found there has proven. Red-earth paintings on the cave walls show men paddling boats and hunting animals and a scene resembling a dance. Boat-shaped coffins from a later date have also been found, which were thought to transport the dead down "the big river" into the next world.

Little is known about the early Niah people, but it is certain that they had developed crafts such as pottery and simple weaving. Pottery and stone implements have been found in Gua Cha, a cave in Kelantan. Fragments of rough boats hauled up into dry shelters show that the early settlers built usable craft using stone tools.

EARLY ASIAN CONTACTS

Strategically located midway between India and China, the Malay Peninsula provides a natural trading interchange between these two giants. It is believed that traders met and exchanged goods in sheltered places along the Straits of Melaka and around the peninsula's southern tip centuries before any ship was prepared to undertake the entire long and dangerous voyage between Calcutta and Shanghai.

Above: **Remains found in Gua Cha indicate that Neolithic migrants from China after 2000 B.C. brought with them an advanced material culture, including pottery of high functional and aesthetic quality.**

Opposite: **A rock painting in the Niah Caves.**

Over the centuries foreign traders and settlers brought their religions and way of life with them, though they did not settle in significant numbers. Hinduism and Buddhism left cultural traces in artifacts and in customs that were absorbed into local folkways. For instance, many Malay wedding customs have their origin in a dim Hindu past. Cheng Hoon Teng, Malaysia's oldest Chinese temple, is dedicated to Admiral Cheng Ho, who visited Melaka in 1405. As more Chinese settled in Malaysia, a unique mix of Chinese and Malay cultures occured, and the Straits Chinese, or Peranakans, were born.

MELAKA

The foundation of the first powerful state in the Straits of Melaka is shrouded in legend. A princeling called Parameswara, exiled from his native Sumatra (now part of Indonesia), set up a pirate base on Temasek (the former name of the island of Singapore). Being a less than popular ruler, he was later expelled and fled to the fishing village of Melaka where he made himself master.

A fortuitous geographic position and the trade patterns of the day assisted Parameswara's undoubted abilities. Melaka grew into a trading center important enough to attract the jealousy of the Siamese, as well as the protection of China, the distant overlord of most of Southeast Asia during that time. Numerous Indian traders settled in Melaka. They brought Islam to the Straits in the early 15th century. The history of Melaka under its Indianized Malay court offers many examples of intrigue and heroism.

Melaka's last chief minister, Tun Mutahir, made the fatal mistake of trying to trick the Portuguese when they sailed into the Straits in 1509. He launched a sneak attack on the foreign vessels in the port. Most of the intruders escaped, only to return with reinforcements to take revenge on the treacherous "Moors," as they called all Muslims.

Porta de Santiago, the only remaining part of the fort the Portuguese built in Melaka.

THE BRITISH PERIOD

The founding of Singapore in 1819 and the Anglo-Dutch Treaty of 1824 gave Britain control of the Straits of Melaka. Labor was imported from India and China to work tin mines and rubber plantations. In the 1870s, local conflicts gave the British an excuse to install "advisors" in the sultans' courts. These British officials ruled the states except for matters of religion and local custom. In 1896, Perak, Pahang, Selangor, and Negeri Sembilan were persuaded to unite as the Federated Malay States for administrative convenience.

The Indian and Chinese communities became more prominent in the 1920s. Anti-British Chinese political parties were founded. Malay nationalism stirred. Each community was suspicious of every other but relied on the British to keep order.

Malaya, as the peninsula was known, consisted of the Federated and Unfederated Malay States under British protection and the Straits Settlements of Penang, Melaka, and Singapore, which were British colonies.

The Japanese invaded Malaya on December 9, 1941, the same day they bombed Pearl Harbor. They surrendered to the Allies, which included the British, in 1945.

WESTERN CONTACTS

Portugal was the first Western nation to raise its flag in the Straits of Melaka. The Portuguese took control of Melaka in 1511 and built a fort, a church, and a customs house.

Things were not rosy for the Portuguese. The exiled sultan of Melaka, having established himself in Johor on the southern tip of the peninsula, was trying to regain his dominion.

Other powerful Malay states in the region resented the Christian intruders' attempts at creating a trade monopoly. Sea rovers and pirates were encouraged to attack foreign shipping vessels. Rather than risk taking the route through the pirate-infested Straits of Melaka, bigger and better-equipped vessels chose to sail west of Sumatra on their way to Batavia in the Dutch East Indies. As a result, legitimate trade declined.

The Dutch, who had established themselves in western Java in the early 17th century, defeated the Portuguese in Melaka in 1641, and the town's importance declined rapidly after the British acquired Penang from the sultan of Kedah in 1786 and Melaka from the Dutch in 1824. Penang became the only important foreign trading base in the Straits.

Chinese traders joined the early settlements to exchange Chinese goods for Indian ones and to buy the peninsula's produce. It is from Chinese historians that we know what goods were in demand, at what prices, and how the people of the Malay Peninsula dressed and behaved.

Above right: **Food rationing in a village affected by Emergency operations. Life did not return to normal after the war in 1945. Guerrillas who had harassed the occupying forces refused to lay down their weapons, striving to replace the colonial government with a communist one.**

In 1948, an emergency was declared. It dragged on for 12 years, holding the country in a state of siege, restricting population movement, free assembly, and many other freedoms usually taken for granted.

Opposite: **Tunku Abdul Rahman, Malaysia's first prime minister, declaring the independence of the federation at a ceremony on August 31, 1957.**

THE INGREDIENTS OF MALAYSIA

The Malaysian Emergency was declared in mid-1948 when the Malayan Communist Party (MCP) embarked on a systematic campaign of violence against European interests. The Communists were mainly Chinese and received substantial support from their rural compatriots. After 1950 British forces gained control by resettling these communities into "New Villages," thus denying the MCP access to supplies. The Emergency officially ended in 1960.

The main reason for the Communist insurrection's failure was a new alliance between Malay and Chinese leaders and Britain's commitment to Malaya's independence. Malaya's first elections were held in 1955, in preparation for independence in 1957. Three parties emerged: the United Malays National Organization (UMNO), the Malayan Chinese Association (MCA), and the Malayan Indian Congress (MIC). The first elected prime minister was from the Kedah aristocracy, Tunku Abdul Rahman.

In the early 1960s, a new, larger federation was proposed: Malaysia, including Malaya and Singapore, and Brunei, Sarawak, and Sabah on the island of Borneo. Brunei, Sarawak, and Sabah became British colonies after World War II. Before that, Sarawak had been ruled by the family of James Brooke, known as the "White Rajahs." Sabah had been ruled by a chartered company founded by the British—the British North Borneo Company—and foreign trade interests.

In the end, Brunei chose not to join the federation. The British government granted Sabah and Sarawak independence through joining the Federation of Malaysia declared in 1963. Singapore left Malaysia in 1965 to become an independent republic.

Postwar Malaysia was marked by the political drive of the Malays, expressed through the UMNO party. But Malay dominance also caused bitterness and racial antagonism, resulting in the deaths of hundreds during the 1969 racial riots in Kuala Lumpur. While just over half of the population was ethnic Malay, only 1.5 percent of company assets in the country were owned by Malays, and per capita income among Malays was less than half that of non-Malays. In light of this, a policy in favor of Malays was introduced in the 1970s to help even up this economic inequality. The Malays and indigenous peoples of Malaysia were offered privileges in business, education, property development, and government, and were classified as *bumiputera* ("boo-MI-put-teh-RAH"), or "sons of the soil." Despite this legislation, the Malays have not yet achieved economic equality with Chinese Malaysians. The policy has caused some resentment among the latter group, who are loath to invest wholeheartedly in a country where they face discrimination.

Like the flag, the coat of arms features a crescent and a 14-point star. The five *keris*, four different colored panels, and left and right divisions represent the peninsular states. The two divisions flanking the national flower, the *bunga raya* ("boong-ngeh rah-yeh"), represent Sabah and Sarawak. The motto, in Roman and *jawi* ("jah-wi") scripts, is "Unity for Progress."

GOVERNMENT

MALAYSIA IS A FEDERAL CONSTITUTIONAL MONARCHY with a nonpolitical head of state known as the *yang di-pertuan agong* ("young di-per-twan ah-gohng"). Each member state has its own legislature. Sabah and Sarawak even have their own immigration laws, so a passport is needed when traveling between East and Peninsular Malaysia.

PARLIAMENT

The federal parliament consists of two chambers, the House of Representatives and the Senate. The representatives are elected by the people; the senators appointed by the *yang di-pertuan agong* or elected by the state legislatures. The parliament is the legislative arm of the government. The party that commands a majority in the parliament chooses the prime minister, or *perdana menteri* ("per-DAH-nah men-teh-ri"), though he is officially appointed by the *yang di-pertuan agong*. The *perdana menteri* chooses his party members in the House of Representatives or Senate to be ministers in charge of various portfolios. This cabinet is responsible to the parliament and ultimately to the electorate. In the United States, one person—the president—fulfills both executive and ceremonial functions. In Malaysia, the two functions are separate: the *perdana menteri* is the chief executive of the nation and the *yang di-pertuan agong* is the ceremonial head of state.

Above: **The installation of Sultan Azlan Shah as the yang di-pertuan agong of Perak in 1989.**

Opposite: **The National Monument, designed by the creator of the Iwo Jima Memorial in Washington, D.C., was constructed in 1966 to commemorate the nation's heroes.**

LOCAL ADMINISTRATION

The smallest administrative unit is the village or—in Sabah and Sarawak—the longhouse. A *ketua kampung* ("keh-twah kahm-pohng"), meaning village elder, or *tuai rumah* ("too-why roo-mah"), meaning house elder, presides over the village or longhouse community. In Chinese-populated areas, a *kapitan Cina* ("kah-pi-tahn chee-nah"), or Chinese elder, is appointed with similar limited functions.

An elder is usually appointed, though elders in the past were elected by the population under their jurisdiction. The rationale for these positions is that a person versed in traditional law and customs should deal with the small, ordinary matters that arise in the daily life of the community. In some ways their functions resemble those of a justice of the peace.

The elder is in charge of the smooth functioning of his community. He directs sanitation projects and other community activities. In most states he can even impose small fines. But he has limited judicial powers to settle family disputes and infringements of traditional law. Most everyday legal matters, such as the issuing of birth, marriage, and death certificates, are handled by the district offices.

An informal discussion between a village elder and some villagers.

The larger towns of Malaysia have town boards, municipal councils, or city councils. These bodies administer planning, sanitation, and building bylaws; issue various licenses and permits; and collect fees for services, including refuse collection and road maintenance.

City and municipal councils may be appointed or elected, the process differing from state to state.

DATUK SERI DR. MAHATHIR MOHAMMED

In 1981 Datuk Seri Dr. Mahathir Mohammed (*right*) became Malaysia's fourth *perdana menteri*. He has a nonaristocratic background and is Malaysia's first *perdana menteri* not educated in the British school system or at a British university. This has led to the emergence of a Malaysia with a less British-oriented outlook.

Though at times considered authoritarian in style by his critics, Mahathir has sought to enhance and strengthen the power of the political executive and limit the powers of the traditional rulers (the *agongs*) and unions. A conflict arose between the government and the *agongs* over the brutal beating of a man who had criticized the Johor royal family in 1992. The incident polarized popular opinion, but the *agongs* did not receive the grassroots support they hoped for. As a result, the government's power increased, and the *agongs* lost many taken-for-granted privileges.

LAW

Malaysians may not hold dual citizenship. Those who do so are liable to lose their Malaysian citizenship by process of law.

A Malaysian father remains the legal guardian of his children even if he has divorced their mother. Non-Muslim Malaysians under 21 years of age cannot get married if their parents object. If these objections are unreasonable, the couple may seek a court order to override their parents' objections or wait until both turn 21. Muslim women can marry once they turn 16; Muslim men after age 18. Muslim marriages must be registered at least a week before the wedding and are solemnized at a mosque.

Under the Internal Security Act, Malaysians may be detained without being charged in court if they are suspected of being a threat to public order or the security of the country. The death penalty is mandatory for persons convicted of drug trafficking, and the criminal is usually executed within a few months of conviction.

Judicial authority in Malaysia is vested in the High Court of Malaya (Peninsular Malaysia) and the High Court of Borneo (Sabah and Sarawak), and in appropriate lower courts. The courts decide civil and criminal cases or settle the legality of any law or act of government that is questioned. To enable it to perform its work impartially, the judiciary is designed to be independent of political or any other interference.

ECONOMY

NEARLY HALF OF MALAYSIA'S POPULATION is rural after almost half a century of rapid rural-to-urban migration. The United Nations Statistics Division put Malaysia's rural-urban population distribution at a ratio of 43:57 in 2000, although the figures for rural dwellers are higher in Sabah and Sarawak. Some 16 percent of the national workforce of 9.3 million people are today engaged in agriculture for a living.

MAIN OCCUPATIONS

The biggest employers in Malaysia are the civil service and the manufacturing sector. The latter includes petroleum refining, car assembly, and the processing of domestic raw materials, such as timber, rubber, and oil.

One important industry is mining. Tin still brings in a portion of Malaysia's foreign exchange earnings. Malaya's oldest known name, Aurea Chersonesus, means peninsula of gold. There is still the occasional gold rush when villagers scramble on river banks, washing mud and sand in wide, flat basins, searching for the precious metal. Crude oil and natural gas are found in offshore fields in the South China Sea. The main oil-producing states are Terengganu in Peninsular Malaysia and Sabah and Sarawak.

The country's long coastline and numerous rivers and lakes present many opportunities for fishing, an important occupation even today.

Above: **Malaysia is the world's fifth-largest producer of tin, after Brazil, China, Indonesia, and Bolivia.**

Opposite: **Collecting sun-dried fish.**

MALAYSIAN INDUSTRIES

Many Malaysian industries process raw materials extracted locally. For instance, home-grown timber is made into furniture, veneer, and plywood for both local and international consumption. Natural gas found in offshore fields in the South China Sea is liquified in Malaysia, and some crude oil is refined locally. Petroleum products, such as chemicals and plastics, are manufactured in Malaysia before being exported.

Malaysia is the world's third largest rubber producer with an average annual rubber output of 900,000 tons. In the first two months of 2000 alone, Malaysia exported 114,379 tons of rubber.

Heavy industry is also growing. Malaysia supports a thriving iron and steel industry and produces its own automobiles. Trucks, tractors, and other heavy vehicles, in demand in rural areas where the roads are poor, are also manufactured domestically.

Malaysia has a large fishing industry employing over 600,000 people and a major food industry mainly for the home market. But it is not yet self-sufficient and still has to import beef, cereals, and other food products to supplement domestic output.

The health of Malaysia's construction industry fluctuates with the economic realities of the day. After being hit by the Asian financial crisis in 1997, the construction industry grew by 3.1 percent in 2000 and contributed 3.4 percent to the gross domestic product.

Malaysia has recently attained newly industrialized economy (NIE) status, having previously relied heavily on agriculture. Coming out of its worst depression in decades after the 1997 financial crisis, the Malaysian

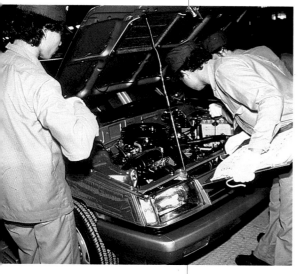

A Proton Saga assembly line. Launched in 1985, the Proton Saga is Malaysia's national car. In late 1993, the Proton Saga set up production operations in Europe, based in Britain. The car is also being imported into South Africa by Malays living there.

economy posted a 5.6 percent growth figure in 1999 and 7.5 percent in 2000. This recovery was driven mainly by export-led manufacturing. Malaysia's long-term goal is to become a developed nation by 2020. The 2020 Vision aims to achieve balanced growth and a high quality of life.

TOURISM

Tourism is Malaysia's third largest foreign exchange earner. The industry contributes around 5 percent to the gross national product. In recent years, Malaysia has developed into one of the region's most popular vacation spots, especially with the improvement of air and land communications.

Many visitors come to enjoy Malaysia's relaxed rural lifestyle, its exotic mix of spicy food, and its excellent swimming and diving spots and uncrowded, unspoiled beaches. Visitors from the cash-rich island Republic of Singapore make up by far the greatest number of tourists to Malaysia each year: thousands of Singaporeans cross the causeway to Johor Bahru on weekends and public holidays.

In 1990 the Malaysian Tourist Promotion Board publicized tourism with a "Visit Malaysia Year" campaign that pulled in 7.4 million visitors and earned the country $1.7 billion in revenue. In 1999 Malaysia launched a new worldwide marketing campaign called "Malaysia, Truly Asia."

The Kuala Lumpur International Airport (KLIA) occupies an area of 24,711 acres (10,000 hectares), making it one of the largest airports in the world.

COTTAGE INDUSTRIES AND RETAIL COMMERCE

In theory, every industry, however small, needs a license in Malaysia. In practice, some cottage industries flourish without much supervision.

A street peddler selling medicines.

Many people from the lower income groups eke out a meager living by hawking, that is, by selling things in the streets. Hawkers may sell cigarettes, soft drinks, secondhand clothing, and other small or factory-rejected goods. Many Malaysian towns have established hawkers' centers, but many hawkers prefer to ply their trade on footpaths, by roadsides, at bus stations, in parking lots, or wherever people congregate. Some street sellers bring their wares in a trishaw, a three-wheeled bicycle; others have a temporary stall to shelter them and their goods from the rain. But many makeshift hawkers carry their goods in baskets or spread their goods on mats on the ground, ready to vanish if anybody objects to their presence or wants to see their license.

Some hawkers have a business license and earn respectable amounts of money. Many of them, however, are fly-by-night operators and take to their heels when they see a policeman approaching. Many Malaysian housewives prepare cakes and snacks for sale and set up small stalls outside their houses. During the Muslim fasting month of *Ramadan* ("rah-mah-dahn"), whole night markets spring up.

The sale of handmade baskets and mats is coordinated by the Handicrafts Development Board. One of Malaysia's most distinctive handicrafts, organized as a small industry in many rural places, is a wax-resistant dyed fabric called *batik* ("bah-tick"). *Batik* material has all kinds of uses in Malaysia, including clothing, tablecloths, and curtains. Good-quality *batik* shirts are considered appropriate dress for men on formal occasions and at celebrations, be they weddings, business meetings, or diplomatic functions.

Batik is produced mainly on the eastern coast of the peninsula, from where it is sold to other parts of Malaysia and to Indonesia, Thailand, and Singapore. Sarawak's Iban people produce a labor-intensive cloth called *ikat* ("ee-kaht"). Before weaving, the threads are dipped in dyes extracted from forest plants—usually black, red, or yellow ochre. The threads are dyed so that abstract geometric shapes or stylized forms of crocodiles, lizards, and snakes only appear when the fabric is woven.

Basket- and mat-weaving are thriving cottage industries coordinated under the Handicrafts Development Board.

ENVIRONMENT

WITH MORE THAN 60 PERCENT of its land covered with rainforest, Malaysia is rich in plant and animal life. The country's forests are home to some 300 species of mammals and 736 species of birds. Around 8,000 species of flowering plants grow in West Malaysia alone. Malaysia also boasts the world's tallest tropical tree and largest flower. The Tualang tree, with a base diameter of over 10 feet (3 m), reaches heights of around 262 feet (80 m). The Rafflesia flower, 3 feet (1 m) wide, holds a Guinness record.

Today, the Malaysian rainforest is under threat. Agriculture, urban development, and other human activities continue to eat into virgin forest, bulldozing valuable trees and destroying animal habitats. Haze from forest fires harms the air, and industrial waste released into rivers poisons marine life. As a result, many animals in Malaysia, such as orangutans, the Sumatran rhinoceros, elephants, tigers, and turtles, are now in danger of extinction. It has been estimated that if the pace of destruction of the rainforest continues, half of all mammals and 25 percent of all bird species in Peninsular Malaysia will cease to exist by 2020.

The Malaysian government, together with world conservation authorities, is taking stern measures to protect the country's endangered wildlife and ensure the preservation of the natural environment for future generations.

Above: **The Rafflesia in full bloom.**

Opposite: **A trekker takes a walk through the forest canopy in the Taman Negara National Park.**

The Malayan Tiger.

ENDANGERED WILDLIFE

THE MALAYAN TIGER Tiger numbers have fallen worldwide due to deforestation and poaching. The bones and other body parts of the tiger are used to make traditional medicines in Asia. In the early 1900s, there were around 100,000 tigers in the world. Today only 5,000 to 7,500 exist. Of the eight original subspecies, only five now survive.

The Indo-Chinese subspecies in Malaysia is commonly called the Malayan tiger. It was once a common sight in Peninsular Malaysia, but urban development has eaten into its living space and reduced its population to around 500. These rare creatures can now be seen only in a few states and in the Taman Negara National Park. No tigers have been reported in Penang and Melaka.

TURTLES Turtles have existed since the Triassic period more than 200 million years ago. Most species, such as the giant Mesozoic sea turtle Archelon, which reached some 8 feet (2.4 m) in diameter, are now extinct. Only seven sea turtle species survive today, all on the endangered list. The Leatherback, Hawksbill, Green, and Olive Ridley sea turtles nest on Malaysian beaches. The largest of these, the Leatherback, is unlikely to escape extinction.

Some causes of the decline in turtle numbers are human consumption of turtle eggs (valued as an aphrodisiac), accidental capture in fishing nets, marine pollution, and the loss of nesting grounds due to human activity in coastal areas. Conservationists try to preserve turtle populations by reburying turtle eggs in hatcheries.

THE SUMATRAN RHINOCEROS The Sumatran rhinoceros is the smallest of its kind, weighing up to 2,205 pounds (1,000 kg). It is a popular target among poachers motivated by a large Asian market for its horns, which are valued as an aphrodisiac.

Sumatran rhinoceroses are the most endangered of all the Asian species. There are probably fewer than 500 in the world, mostly in Indonesia. Those in Malaysia live in the Endau-Rompin reserve in Sabah. Captive breeding is the only hope for the survival of this species, until adequate protection can be provided in the wild.

THE MALAYAN ELEPHANT The Malayan elephant is a subspecies of the Asian elephant. Asian elephants are found mainly in reserves in India and Southeast Asia. They have smaller tusks than their African counterparts and are thus not as intensively poached for ivory. Their decline has been mainly due to the destruction of their natural habitat. Domesticated elephants are often used to clear their own native homes to make way for agriculture.

THE ORANGUTAN

The orangutan (*right*) is man's closest relative and Asia's only great ape. It is extremely intelligent, but is sadly one of the most endangered of Malaysian wildlife species. There are less than 30,000 orangutans alive in the world today. Found only in Borneo and Sumatra, the animal's survival is constantly threatened by forest fires, logging, and poaching. The Sepilok Orangutan Sanctuary in Sabah—24,711 acres (10,000 hectares) of virgin rainforest—gives orangutans space to roam and mate, free from human interference.

CURRENT ISSUES

WATER POLLUTION Urbanization and industrialization are adding to the demand for clean water and yet at the same time polluting Malaysia's natural water sources. Cleaning up polluted waterways is an urgent task, as 90 percent of Malaysia's water supply comes from lakes, rivers, and streams flowing from the highland forests.

Malaysia's water pollution problem started in the 1970s with the birth of the palm oil processing industry. Factories released industrial waste into rivers, polluting the water and killing marine life. The continued expansion of industry means that Malaysia's natural waterways will never be safe from industrial pollutants. Domestic sewage discharge, land clearing, and livestock farming also contribute to water pollution in Malaysia.

AIR POLLUTION According to the Department of Environment (DOE), 8.9 million motor vehicles registered in 1998 emitted approximately 2 million tons of carbon monoxide, 237,000 tons of nitrogen oxides, 111,000 tons of hydrocarbons, and 38,000 tons of sulfur dioxide. The same year, the DOE launched a nationwide surveillance program to prevent open burning activities. Within nine months, patrol teams found 495 cases.

Motor vehicles, industry, land clearing, and open burning have caused serious air pollution problems in Malaysia. In 1997, smoke billowing from 11 million acres (4.5 million hectares) of burning forest in Sumatra,

Kalimantan, and Borneo left several countries in Southeast Asia breathing noxious air for months. The number of cases of respiratory disease more than doubled in Kuala Lumpur, while in Sarawak, airports, offices, factories, shops, and schools were closed, and the town's residents were advised to stay home or wear protective masks.

Besides intensifying respiratory ailments, the haze may have long-term effects. Incomplete combustion of organic matter, such as trees and fossil fuels, releases polycyclic aromatic hydrocarbons (PAHs) into the atmosphere. The haze caused by raging forest fires in Indonesia in 1997 exposed people to PAHs, some of which can cause cancer. When industrial and traffic emissions mix with PAHs, the overall effect can be lethal.

DEFORESTATION Malaysia is one of the 10 top exporters of timber in the world. The import of tropical hardwoods by industrialized nations has increased 15 times since 1950. As the most populous nations become wealthier, they will add even more to the global consumption of wood products. To meet this growing demand, timber-exporting countries like Malaysia have been depleting their forest cover at an alarming rate. This rapid deforestation has contributed to land degradation—the wearing down of the soil and depletion of its nutrients. Deforestation removes vegetation cover and makes topsoil prone to erosion, leading to mudslides, silting, and flooding. Manmade changes in the forest canopy also alter the forest climate and the growth and diversity of trees and animals.

Oil palm plantations contribute significantly to land degradation in Malaysia. Oil palms are planted in neat rows with wide gaps in between, and rain falling on the exposed ground washes away the topsoil. Also, oil palms remain economically viable for 15 years on average, after which they have to be replaced. Repeated planting of oil palms depletes the soil of certain nutrients until eventually it loses its fertility.

Opposite: **A river in Sarawak. Projects to restore polluted rivers are in progress, the largest being the 10-year restoration of the Kelang River.**

ENVIRONMENTAL PROTECTION

The Department of Environment under the Ministry of Science, Technology, and Environment works to fight pollution by studying the environment, monitoring sources of pollutants, and educating Malaysians and involving them in efforts to preserve the environment. The DOE penalizes factories that discharge excessive amounts of effluents and owners of motor vehicles that emit excessive amounts of exhaust fumes, and involves nongovernmental organizations (NGOs) and the private sector in public awareness programs.

The Department of Wildlife and National Parks (DWNP) protects the flora and fauna in Peninsular Malaysia. It manages the Taman Negara National Park and the Sepilok Orangutan Sanctuary. The DWNP has carried out a successful captive breeding program for tigers in the Melaka Zoo, where 30 cubs have been born to tigers once living in the wild.

A path through the protected forest of the Taman Negara National Park.

The Department of Fisheries under the Ministry of Agriculture takes care of Malaysia's marine heritage. This department oversees the management of several marine parks, where efforts are made to protect marine ecosystems, especially coral reefs, for the purposes of research, education, and eco-tourism. The Ma' Daerah and Rantau Abang marine reserves operating under the fisheries department's wing are dedicated to protecting sea turtles. The beaches of Rantau Abang are regularly visited by Leatherback turtles seeking a place to lay their eggs.

Malaysia's environmental conservation efforts are having moderate success. There are stable populations of endangered animals in the national parks and wildlife sanctuaries. Keeping the environment healthy and clean has also benefitted tourism. Visitors come from all over the world to experience Malaysia's diverse culture and admire its beautiful natural environment.

A wildlife protection worker tags a nesting sea turtle at the Selingan Turtle Island Park in Malaysia.

MALAYSIANS

HISTORY AND GEOGRAPHY have collaborated to make Malaysia a truly multiracial country. In the jungle areas of Borneo and the peninsula, shy aboriginal peoples live in traditional ways or reluctantly adapt to life in settlements. Starting around 4000 B.C., succeeding waves of ethnic Malays arrived from the northwest, and aboriginal peoples moved deeper into the interior of the country. Most Chinese settlement occurred in the 19th and early 20th centuries, apart from the few Chinese who landed in the 14th and 15th centuries in Melaka and later Penang. Of over 21 million Malaysians today, 58 percent are Malay and indigenous people, 26 percent Chinese, 7 percent Indian, and 9 percent Eurasian, European, and other minorities.

ORANG ASLI

The aboriginal peoples of Malaysia are called Orang Asli in the peninsula and Penan in Sarawak. They consist of about 20 different tribal populations, numbering more than 90,000. Traditionally they lived by hunting and gathering, staying in rough shelters for a few weeks at a time and then moving on. The last generation of true nomads is middle-aged. Many Orang Asli now live more settled lives as farmers. The men still go off for the occasional jungle trek, but they come back to a strongly built house they are learning to call home.

Above: **Malaya saw a huge influx of Chinese and Indian migrants at the turn of the 19th century, when local mines and plantations needed more labor than the country could provide.**

Opposite: **The streets of Malaysia showcase a multiracial population.**

RURAL MALAY SETTLEMENT

Many Peninsular Malays trace their origins to Sumatra, some having immigrated within the last 50 years. Borneo Malays also have ancestors from that island or from Johor. A Malay village is called a *kampung* ("kahm-pohng"), a group of single-family houses built by preference in the shelter of a river mouth. Fishing is still the main economic activity of rural Malays; fish is one of their favorite foods.

Every Malay *kampung* has its own mosque—called a *masjid* ("mahs-jid")—or at least a *surau* ("soo-rao")—a Muslim house of prayer. In the more populated areas of Malaysia, where people of different races live together, the Malay section of a village is often separated from the Chinese bazaar by a small body of water or river to make sure no pigs (taboo to Muslims) will invade the *kampung*.

LAND DEVELOPMENT PROJECTS

In rural Malaysia, land development projects cover huge areas of land with oil palm, rubber, cocoa, and other cash crops. Houses for the settlers are usually provided by the developer.

Unlike in a traditional *kampung*, houses in a development project are uniform in design and spread out. Each unit includes a small plot of land for growing vegetables or rearing a few chickens. Houses are provided with basic sanitation, water, and electricity. There is also usually a school, a rural clinic, and a few stores.

EAST MALAYSIAN SETTLEMENTS

The longhouse is the traditional dwelling of some indigenous peoples in Sabah and Sarawak. The longhouse is a row of 12 to 50 or even more houses built side by side, so that each house shares a wall with the immediate neighbor on either side. The "village street" is a wide, covered veranda running along the front of the longhouse. Longhouses were built to protect the community. The foundation pillars rose up to 20 feet (6 m) high, and the notched log that served as a staircase was pulled up at night.

While some people have started leaving the longhouse for *kampung*- or urban-style housing, many Borneans still prefer their traditional dwelling. Subsidized public housing in agricultural development areas in Sarawak may be "*kampung*-type" or "longhouse-type," as the settlers wish—and many Borneans prefer a modern longhouse of hewn timber, with glass windows and indoor plumbing.

Above left: **A longhouse.**

Above: **The veranda of a longhouse.**

URBAN COMMUNITY

Malaysia is still a predominantly rural country, but the picture is changing rapidly. *Kampung* or longhouse people move into town for a variety of reasons. They hope to find better schools for their children and better medical and other public facilities. Also educated young people look for employment in towns. Urban housing in Malaysia resembles that in other countries. Terrace houses line the roads in most towns, and condominiums are becoming common in the larger towns. Less planned are the squatter settlements in the urban fringes. Migrants from the villages build shacks out of readily available materials and live in their flimsy shelters temporarily— or so they hope—until they can afford proper housing.

Stone shophouses in Kuala Lumpur's Chinatown. The family business occupies the lower floor, while the upper floor serves as the living quarters.

MALAYSIAN FASHION

Malaysians wear summer clothes all year round. Although urban homes and offices are often air-conditioned, nobody needs sweaters.

Malaysian men wear Western-style shirts and trousers on a daily basis, while Malaysian women wear Western-style dresses, blouses, and skirts. They may put on a suit if their position at work demands it.

Many Malay women wear modern versions of the *baju kurung* (bah-joo koo-rohng"), a flowing knee-length blouse worn over an ankle-length skirt. Indian women are often seen in a gossamer *sari* ("SAH-ri"), a 6-yard (5.5-m) length of material wrapped gracefully around their body. Their Sikh counterparts wear a *shalwar-kameez* ("shehl-WAHR kheh-MEEZ"), a knee-length blouse worn over baggy trousers of the same material. Sikhs are Punjabi Indians who follow the teachings of Guru Nanak, the founder of Sikhism.

While the classical high-necked, side-slit Chinese *cheongsam* ("chee-OHNG-sahm") is not much in fashion now, the *sam foo* ("sahm-foo") suit of a fitted floral blouse and matching pants is worn by many women who work at food stands and similar occupations. It looks smart and is practical.

Left: High school students in their white blouses and turquoise jumpers, and Muslim schoolgirls in their white baju kurung and long skirt.

Below: A Sikh schoolboy with his long hair combed into a tight silk-wrapped topknot. The Sikh religion forbids the cutting of hair for both men and women.

All Malaysian schoolchildren wear the same uniforms. For elementary-school students it is white and navy. High-school girls wear a white blouse and turquoise jumper, while the boys wear white shirts and army-green pants. Many Muslim schoolgirls may wear a white *baju kurung* over a long turquoise skirt. The more traditional among them swathe their heads in scarves or white veils worn over tight-fitting caps. They are not allowed to cover their faces—the education authorities want to be quite sure that the person taking an examination is the candidate herself, and not somebody else!

Muslim women may cover their heads with a veil, although this is not considered necessary for ordinary purposes. It is compulsory only for attending the mosque or saying prayers at home. The very orthodox follow a recently imported fashion of covering their faces in public, known as *purdah* ("PERH-dah"). Muslim men cover their heads when engaged in devotions, wearing a rimless black hat called *songkok* ("sohng-koh"), which may also be worn for everyday purposes.

Sikh boys from conservative families wear their hair uncut and formed into a tight topknot wrapped in a silk handkerchief. Their elder brothers and fathers wear the traditional turban, made up of 30 feet (9 m) of fine muslin wound over a loose-fitting cap. Sikh women should wear a veil when going outdoors, but this restriction is not taken too seriously by the younger generation.

HOLIDAY WEAR AND TRADITIONAL COSTUMES

Indian and Malay women often wear their traditional clothes on weekdays and to work. For holidays, all Malaysians make an effort to look sharp: appearing at a festival in shabby clothes is considered disrespectful to the host and to the occasion.

Malay boys and girls are usually dressed up in miniature versions of the traditional Malay costumes worn by their parents. The children usually behave with the utmost gravity at ceremonies.

Chinese children may be dressed in traditional robes or trouser-suits for the Chinese New Year, but this is more common for girls. Few boys above the age of 6 would care to be seen in silk pajamas and a red-buttoned hat by their schoolfriends!

East Malaysians bring out their festive costumes for holiday occasions. Most of these are colorful and picturesque, tradition combined with modern additions like shiny satin, glittering sequins, paper flowers, and—the very latest—aluminum-foil imitations of priceless heirloom jewelry. This substitution is popular when costuming schoolchildren for concerts and other performances. If the real antique silver was lost or damaged, the loss could run into thousands of dollars.

Chinese children may dress in traditional robes for the Chinese New Year.

LIFESTYLE

"A MALAYSIAN RUNS INTO A CLINIC with blood stains on his head. He inquires after the doctor's health, not forgetting grandma, grandpa, and the rest of the doctor's family. After a few remarks about the weather, he finally tells the doctor that he has had a little problem with a brick falling off a building ..."

This story, though exaggerated, has a germ of truth in it. Malaysians are a reserved people, given to ceremonious politeness that may seem pointless to a non-Asian observer.

For Malaysians, rules of behavior must be carefully observed within the family and one's own circle of friends, although "people we don't know" somehow fall outside this requirement.

There are personal disagreements between parents and children from time to time, but nobody seriously doubts that their elders' blessings, however formalized, are necessary for them to have "good future, prosperity, health, and long life," to quote a common Malaysian congratulatory formula.

Malay children kiss their parents' hands and beg their forgiveness on Hari Raya Puasa, the celebration of the end of Ramadan, the Muslim fasting month. The practice of kissing the hands of their elders is called *salam* ("sah-lahm"). Chinese children pay their respects to their elders on Chinese New Year by offering them Mandarin oranges and kneeling to receive their blessings.

This may seem quaint to foreigners, but the parties involved see nothing strange in it. On the other hand, many Malaysians are embarrassed to see people hug and kiss in public, as is common among Westerners. "I blush just to see them," comments an elderly Malay about Western tourists greeting friends at the airport, "in front of everybody, too ..."

STRONG FAMILY TIES

Traditionally most Malaysians lived within easy reach of their close relatives. Villagers were likely to find marriage partners within their own or a neighboring community. Any joyous or sad event was shared with a big crowd of cousins, aunts, and uncles. However small a house, there is always room for a relative to stay for a few days… or a few weeks… or a few years!

Traditionally, children do not set up home on their own after marriage. Rather an extension to the house is built to accommodate the new-lyweds. The extended household is usually big and noisy with grand-parents, siblings and their spouses, and many grandchildren.

It never fails to astonish Malaysians when foreign friends casually admit that they do not know all their own second cousins. Malaysians, whether Malay, Chinese, or Indian, certainly do. And they know what to call them: elder cousin, younger cousin, eldest aunt, youngest uncle. Names are not much used within the family context; everyone is addressed by their family "status." A baby is called "worm," or something similar, to protect it from the jealousy of evil spirits.

Recent immigrants have maintained their family connections with the "old country," be it China, India, or Sumatra. Some conservative Indian parents make sure their children marry into a suitable family by contacting a matchmaker in the Indian subcontinent to arrange a match for a son or daughter. These arrangements do not always come to fruition. Young Malaysians may have different ideas from what their parents hope for their future, although they usually feel bad about disobeying their parents on so important a subject.

Most Malaysian societies have ritualized the in-law relationship. Rudeness to the in-laws is unforgivable. Even a person who does not like his mother-in-law much would consider Western jokes on the topic in very bad taste.

BIRTH—RITES AND TABOOS

Malaysian women share a deep concern for their married daughters' and granddaughters' welfare. Great care is given to the protection of pregnant women and newborn babies from all harm.

The father-to-be has to watch his step too. In some communities, he is not allowed to kill anything, not even a snake, because it is believed that such an act would scar the unborn baby. Pregnant and newly delivered mothers keep away from the cold and wind. They do not consume "cold" foods like vegetables, fruit, and iced drinks. And to shelter from the wind, they cover their heads with a piece of cloth.

For 40 days after delivery, Chinese mothers are fed chicken soup with wine and herbs in order to keep them warm. For the same number of days, they cannot shampoo their hair, no matter how hot and sticky they may feel. They also cannot take their newborn out for fear the wind would harm the child.

Many modern women refuse to be hampered by such taboos, although they may pretend to go along with them so as not to offend their elders. They may put up with the soup for a week or so, then get a friend to smuggle fresh fruit into the house!

Malay babies have their heads ceremonially shaved when they are 40 days old, at the time the mother's confinement ends. Some are also taught to "tread the ground" at this age. Since they are still far too young to walk, their tiny feet are brushed gently against the ground, or a handful of earth is held against the soles of their feet.

Whenever possible, a Malay baby is breastfed, as it is believed that this fosters a strong spiritual bond between mother and child.

GROWING UP IN MALAYSIA

Above: **Malay children have a carefree childhood.**

Below: **A Malay boy goes to a Koran teacher to learn Muslim scripture.**

Kampung and longhouse children have a carefree childhood, while their fellows on a Chinese farm or in a shophouse are expected to help at home from an early age. A Malay or Dayak boy can play by the water with his friends and run home for a snack or a nap when it suits him, while his sister helps mother with household chores. He may go fishing and add his catch to the family meal, but nobody tells him to do so.

Few Malaysian children are told to do much of anything, not even when to go to bed. At all-night parties or ceremonies, they are often found observing the proceedings or dropping off to sleep in a corner.

At 5 or 6, Malay boys are sent to a Koran teacher to learn Muslim scripture. They have to master Arabic writing, then words and sentences, then whole chapters of the Holy Book. Malay girls, too, are proficient in the art of Koran reading. The boys cover their head with a *songkok*; the girls wear a muslin veil when handling or reading the Koran.

A party is held when a boy has finished studying the Holy Book. Dressed in his best and supervised by his proud teachers and parents, he has to give a public recital of his accomplishment.

At the age of 10 to 12, after they have completed reading the Koran, Malay boys are circumcised as their religion demands. Circumcision used to be a semipublic event that involved a feast for the whole *kampung*. Nowadays the minor operation is performed by a doctor, in the privacy of his office. The family may give a meal to celebrate the safe completion of this rite, inviting close relatives only.

Girls are circumcised too, but not in the drastic fashion prevalent in some parts of Africa. A slight nick, usually administered by the child's mother or the village midwife, satisfies the demands of Muslim tradition.

A Malay girl wears a veil over her head when handling or reading the Koran.

COMMON CHILDHOOD TABOOS

A baby should not be praised or called fat, as this may attract the attention of evil spirits. Similarly whistling in the dark will attract evil spirits.

One should not look at a baby through a mirror or the baby will drown later in life.

One should not talk to a baby from the head of his cradle, as this will make him cross-eyed.

Children should not sit on bed pillows or they will get boils on their buttocks.

Children learning to write should not eat chicken feet or their handwriting will become crabbed like the scratches made by a chicken's claws.

In Malaysian schools, classes are fairly large—about 50 students to a class—and discipline is strict. Many schools run two sessions with half the school population attending classes in the morning and the other half in the afternoon. This maximizes the use of limited facilities.

GOING TO SCHOOL

Malaysian children begin elementary school at the age of 6. Classes are fairly large and strictly disciplined. Each child sits at his or her desk during normal lesson time and has to learn a lot of material by heart.

Malaysian schoolchildren wear uniforms. Girls are not allowed to wear jewelry, makeup, colorful socks and shoes, or hair ribbons in any color other than their uniform colors. Boys must keep their hair short. If their hair is long enough to touch the top of their shirt collar at the back, they may face disciplinary action.

In most Malaysian schools, students have to stand up when answering a question. When a teacher enters the classroom, the students rise and greet the teacher in chorus, "*Selamat pagi, cikgu*" ("Seh-lah-maht pah-gi, cheh-goo"), meaning "Good morning, teacher." In rural areas, secondary schools have large boarding houses for students who live far away. They only go home for holidays.

Rather than leave their mothers for boarding school, some girls in the rural areas opt to stay at home after they have completed elementary school. Some old-fashioned parents do not allow their daughters to leave, insisting that she needs to learn housekeeping, rather than trigonometry, to prepare her for her future role as wife and mother.

WOMEN AT HOME

Within most ordinary Malaysian households, the wife and mother reigns supreme. She is the first to say that the father is the head of the family—outside the home. He may make the big family decisions, he may buy the car, he may own the house. But nobody dares to dispute the woman's executive powers inside the house.

The mother does more than manage the house and the lives of her family members. She also handles the family finances and is the final authority on exactly what proportion of the family's income will be spent on education, what the best career is for each of her children, and where to invest the family's savings. She probably even decides how much money her husband can spend on the car he proudly buys and owns. And she is likely to know about her grown-up son's marriage plans before her husband finds out.

Many married women work in low-paying jobs to supplement the family income. Only a better education can help enhance women's job prospects and earning power.

While Malaysian women are powerful within the family, they have yet to make an impact on the young country's public life, either in government or in the business world. At the beginning of the 21st century, there were only two women ministers and one woman deputy minister in the Cabinet. Women are still not represented in many state legislatures.

Theoretically Malaysian women have equal rights with men, including equal access to education and employment. In practice, however, families with limited funds spend their money on their sons, who will have to work for a living one day. Families seldom insist on their daughters being as well-educated as their sons, expecting that the girls will be supported by their future husbands.

COURTSHIP

In Malaysia, a person at age 21 is free to choose his or her marriage partner. How do Malaysians find their soul mates? As few teenagers in the towns own cars, most go out in groups and take the bus. By the time they enter college, many have paired up and are beginning to think about marriage and starting their own families. Living together without first getting married is almost unheard of in Malaysia, and having children out of wedlock risks the couple being excluded from the community.

Young people seldom go on dates but meet in groups in public places

What is considered acceptable dating behavior in towns may be objectionable in the eyes of country folk. Generally, kissing in public is out of the question. A young couple walking hand-in-hand in town may simply attract an occasional frown from a passer-by; in a seaside *kampung*, this emotional display is seen to be too explicit.

In rural areas, many girls are betrothed at infancy and may marry by age 15. It is likely that if she does well in school, she will go to college. But if she fails the exams, she will get married.

Some Indian families look for spouses from India for their children. A matchmaker, considering the history and the social and economic position of the family, draws up horoscopes of possible partners. Many happily married middle-aged Indian couples never met before their wedding day! A bride is expected to be a virgin; conservative in-laws may make her life unpleasant if she is not. A young man, however, is not as seriously expected to restrain himself before marriage.

MARRIAGE

Even among people of the same race and religion, marriage ceremonies may vary from region to region. Those described here are the most common in Malaysia.

MALAY WEDDINGS Even if a young man has chosen his future wife, his parents have to "obtain" his bride for him. Senior relatives visit the woman's house to inquire whether the young lady is still free (meaning unbetrothed). If the reply is encouraging, both sides fix an auspicious day for the betrothal and agree on the dowry and share of expenses. Other gift items exchanged may include a ring, a complete trousseau, good quality cloth (like silk), a complete betel-nut set, cakes, and fruit.

Gorgeously arrayed, bride and groom sit side by side on decorated chairs. The wedding guests come forward to congratulate and bless them by sprinkling rose water, rice grains, and sandalwood paste on the couple's hands. This is called the bersanding ("behr-sahn-ding") and concludes the Malay wedding ceremonies.

The woman is then informed by her mother that she is to become a bride. She must act surprised even if the man is her heart's choice! On the other hand, few Malay women nowadays would marry a man they do not like just because their parents have accepted him. Most parents have also adapted to the younger generation's ways by consulting their child before a response is returned.

The engagement may be held several months before the wedding, or on the day before the ceremony. It is announced to make a family agreement public.

The essential part of a Muslim marriage is the bridegroom's declaration to his new father-in-law that he will provide for his wife and treat her well. This is done before mosque officials and other witnesses. After he has done so to everyone's satisfaction—he may be made to repeat it if it was not loud enough—he is led to "sit in state" beside his bride.

REGIONAL MALAY WEDDING CUSTOMS

The engagement ring is placed on the fourth finger of the bride's right hand by a senior female relative of the groom.

A few weeks before the wedding, the accepted suitor spends a night at his bride-to-be's home. After he has left, the bride-to-be and her sisters search for gifts of gold hidden in the bedding of the room in which he slept.

The day before the wedding, bride and groom have their hands and feet stained red with henna. The bride's hair is trimmed by an elderly female attendant called Mak Andam.

The bridegroom is denied entry into the bride's house by a champion. One of his entourage has to "fight" his way up the steps. The best man "bribes" the women of the household to permit the groom access to the inner rooms.

After the *bersanding*, the bride and groom have to feed each other morsels of sweetened rice. This is hilariously messy, but with Mak Andam's help they manage and the wedding feast can begin.

The morning after the wedding, the couple are made to sit on the back steps. Water is poured over them through a cloth. In the southern state of Johor this leads to a free-for-all splashing party.

CHINESE WEDDINGS The splendid old-fashioned wedding ceremonies of the Malaysian Chinese are the subject of museum exhibits today. Malaysian Chinese who are Christians marry in a church. Others opt for marriage at the clan temple or the registry office.

One tradition still observed is the "engagement sweet." The girl's parents order large quantities of a special sweet that is wrapped in red paper and labeled with the engaged couple's names. This is then sent to all relatives and friends to announce the forthcoming wedding.

The color red—in the form of red paper, red banners, and red decorations—plays a prominent part in all Chinese weddings, traditional, church, or registry. The invitations are printed on red cards, and guests bring a present of money in a red envelope. Red signifies luck.

Even modern families observe some old-fashioned customs, the most important being the tea ceremony in which the bride offers tea to her parents-in-law. Acceptance of the tea offered is acceptance of the daughter-in-law into the family.

At the tea ceremony, the bride and groom first offer tea to the groom's parents and then to the elders of the family, including uncles, aunts, and older siblings of the groom.

Other customs are observed for the fun of it. One such tradition is that only the bride's younger brother can open the groom's car door. When the groom arrives, the boy cannot be found and has to be noisily searched for. Then he proves clumsy with the door handle. A large "bribe," usually a sum of money wrapped in red paper, suddenly improves his skills, and he then lets his future elder brother-in-law out of the car with many respectful bows.

HINDU WEDDINGS Traditionally the first time a Hindu couple met was at their wedding. Modern Hindu couples are more likely to have established a relationship before the wedding.

Three essential ceremonies mark a Hindu wedding: the married women of the family plant a sacred pipal (fig) tree for the couple; the father of the bride gives his daughter away by putting her hand in the bridegroom's; and instead of a wedding ring, the bridegroom fixes a gold *thali* ("taah-li"), or pendant, around the bride's neck as a sign that she is legally his wife. The newly married couple then pace seven times around a flame sacred to the fire god Agni. The bride's veil is tied to the groom's sash to symbolize that "the knot has been tied." The officiating priest throws butter, rice, and flowers into the fire.

The morning after the wedding, the young husband stains the part in his wife's hair with vermilion powder, symbolizing her new status. From now on, the young wife wears gold earrings, necklaces, bangles, and rings, as befits a married woman—only a widow goes unadorned.

A Hindu wedding.

SIKH WEDDINGS In former days, the Sikh bride was wrapped in a long white cloth and carried to the groom by her brothers. The modern Sikh bride walks on her own, suitably escorted. She wears a veil and a red and gold *shalwar-kameez*, the traditional dress for Sikh women. Her groom is likely to wear a Western-style suit.

The bride and groom, surrounded by family and friends, take their vows in front of the Sikh Holy Book, the Adi Granth. To conclude the ceremony, the groom leads the bride four times around the Adi Granth.

WORKING LIFE

Most young Malaysians start looking for jobs after nine to 13 years of formal education. Children ages 6 to 16 enjoy free compulsory education. Attendance is 99 percent at elementary school and 82 percent at secondary school. Almost 3 percent of elementary school students eventually make it to the university.

The Malaysian government gives high priority to education, but places in institutions of higher learning—including about nine universities—are still limited and competition is stiff. The literacy rate in Malaysia has risen above 93 percent of the population since 1998.

Young Malaysians entering the workforce tend to prefer jobs in the government sector; young Malaysian women usually stay on at their workplace after marriage. Once the babies arrive, however, the working mother has to decide whether to continue working and rely on a relative or an *amah* ("ah-mah")—a paid housemaid—to look after the children or to give up her job and stay home to mind the little ones.

Many Malaysian couples can count on a grandmother, aunt, or some other relative to help mind their baby when they go out to work. In many households, the *amah* becomes an important family member, taking the place of the mother. For couples who are not blessed with family members who can take care of their children and who cannot afford to pay a maid, the wife may have to stay home. Day-care facilities at the workplace are not common, and it is unheard of for husbands to give up their jobs and stay at home with the children.

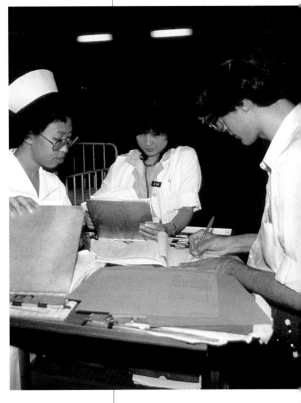

More and more young people are moving away from plantations, farms, and small towns in search of better jobs, better wages, and a better life in the cities.

HAVING FUN

Malaysians like to get together in large numbers to enjoy festivals and public occasions. It is warm enough all year round for everything to be celebrated outdoors, making some allowance for rain.

Malaysians love to picnic in large groups on the beach or by a mountain stream, suitably equipped with guitars and portable hi-fis.

Video is as popular in Malaysia as elsewhere in the world, but it has not put neighborhood movie theaters out of business. Malaysians like to be in a crowd—grannies, babies, the entire family come out to see the latest movies. Young couples find the comparative privacy of a movie theater more appealing than watching the same movie on television at home, surrounded by inquisitive little siblings.

Live sporting events never fail to attract huge crowds. To secure good seats, spectators arrive several hours before the game or match is scheduled to begin. Fans can be sure that hundreds of little food and drink stands will surround the stadium, enabling them to have a picnic while watching the players. Malaysia's favorite sport is soccer, but basketball, tennis, badminton, and, recently, rugby also have devoted followers.

Temple occasions, such as a god's birthday, are celebrated with a procession that draws a crowd instantly. A ritual firewalker or a sword swallower never lacks an audience any more than a cockfight, a quack medicine seller, or a traffic accident does.

Chinese Malaysians are ardent gamblers and a favorite pastime is *mahjong* ("mah-johng"). This is an ancient Chinese game with four players and is similar to many Western card games, except that it uses tiles instead of cards.

POVERTY

The official figure for Malaysian households living in poverty has fallen from 14 percent in 1993 to 5.5 percent in 2000. Real average per capita income was US$10,619 in 2000.

But poverty and income inequality are still a serious problem. Rural poverty is about three times greater than urban poverty. The most impoverished groups are the farmers and fishermen. But as most of them get some of their daily sustenance directly from their work, their situation may not be as bad as the numbers suggest.

Poverty in the towns is manifested in street beggars, many of whom are handicapped. Blind beggars near the entrance of a mosque hope to receive alms from the faithful as they enter to pray. In the larger towns, there is the *jaga kereta* (JAH-gah keh-ray-TAH"), or car-minder, who instead of tending to parked cars, threatens to scratch them unless the owners give him an adequate tip! If they do not cause trouble, beggars are tolerated. An exception are child beggars, forced to beg by their "owners," who may have bought them from their parents. Such children are placed in orphanages by welfare authorities.

The government aims to eradicate hard-core poverty by the end of the decade. About 32 percent of government expenditure has been devoted to the provision of social services, including education and healthcare. The government is also focusing efforts on providing the very poor with free housing and food and small grants and agriculture extension programs to support their income. Needy children are put into nutritional programs, awarded scholarships, and given free textbooks.

Child beggars are not an uncommon sight in Malaysia.

DEATH RITES

When someone dies, as many family members as possible congregate in the home of the bereaved. Since the hot and humid climate necessitates the quick burial or cremation of the dead, not everyone is able to make it to the funeral in time. Many cultures observe rites on certain days after the funeral so that those who could not attend the funeral are able to pay their respects.

A Muslim cemetery where simple headstones mark the graves.

MUSLIM Muslims immediately inform the local mosque officials when somebody has "passed away" (the word *died* is avoided by most Malaysians). The body is washed and shrouded. Only the face is left free and is covered with a fine muslin cloth, which relatives may reverently lift for one last look. Until the funeral, which usually takes place before sunset the same day, family and friends keep vigil.

Before burial, the body is fully shrouded, placed on a bier or in a coffin, and taken to the cemetery. Family members would by then have dug the grave. The body is taken out of the coffin and gently placed in the earth. The call to prayer is recited in the deceased's ear, after which the grave is filled in.

A religious official, protected by an umbrella, recites prayers over the new grave. Flowers, sandalwood shavings, and water are strewn over the raw earth.

Orthodox Islam disapproves of tombstones. In Malaysia, however, hardwood or stone grave markers are common and inscribed headstones not unknown.

CHINESE Wealthy Chinese spend a lot of money on a "respectable" funeral. Economy at such a time would be severely criticized by relatives and friends.

A traditional Chinese coffin is hewn out of the trunk of one hardwood tree, a very expensive receptacle. The body is wrapped in many layers of silk gauze and placed in the coffin. Once the heavy coffin is sealed, it may be kept in the house for several days until all preparations are ready.

Buddhist monks are invited to chant hymns, and members of the deceased's clan association or family serve tea to mourners, keep a record of gifts presented, and generally act as undertakers.

The funeral procession leaves the house at a predetermined time, often 2 P.M. Direct descendants are dressed in shapeless garments of unbleached calico or indigo cotton. The cortege is supposed to walk to the burial site (cremation is becoming common). If it is more than a mile (1.6 km) away, the bereaved family arranges for buses to transport the mourners from a certain point along the route.

At the cemetery, the bereaved family presents each person with a new handkerchief that has a red thread sewn into one of the corners. Upon leaving the graveyard, this cloth should be waved over one shoulder so that spirits cannot follow the mourners.

Some wealthy Chinese mourners engage young male singers whose high-pitched voices are perfect for the sorrowful funeral songs.

INDIAN Sikhs and some non-Muslim Indians cremate their dead. This used to be done on an open-air funeral pyre, where tradition demanded that the deceased's son or other close male relative light the fire. Modern crematoria are now available in Malaysia's main towns.

RELIGION

MALAYSIA IS A LAND OF DIVERSE FAITHS. The country's oldest indigenous religion is animism, where the object of worship is nature. The devoted believe that animals, plants, and natural phenomena like the weather are imbued with spirits. The interior tribes of Peninsular Malaysia—the Orang Asli—and some tribal groups in Borneo are animists, or were so until quite recently.

Hinduism, Buddhism, and Islam reached Malaysia from India and China. In the early days of the Melaka kingdom, the court was influenced by Indian Hindu beliefs. Islam is generally thought to have arrived in Melaka in the 15th century, though recent discoveries may push that date back significantly.

The first Christian church in Malaysia was built by the Portuguese in Melaka. More Christian missionaries arrived in the late 19th century. They never attempted to convert the Muslims, devoting their labors to the "pagans" instead.

Above: **The Terengganu Stone, inscribed with** *jawi* **script, suggests that Islam had arrived in Terengganu by 1303.**

Opposite: **The oldest mosque in Kuala Lumpur, Masjid Jamek, was built in 1909 in the style of northern Indian mosques.**

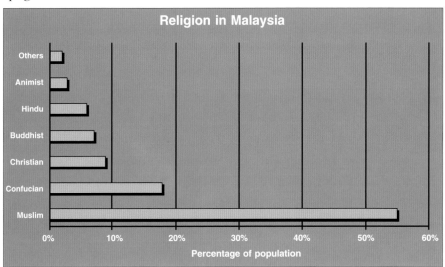

Religion in Malaysia

Percentage of population

67

ISLAM

Islam is a Middle Eastern religion based on the revelations of Prophet Mohammed in the fifth century A.D.

Muslims are obliged to profess their faith, pray five times a day, pay a tithe of their income to the mosque, fast during the month of *Ramadan*, and make a pilgrimage to Mecca once in their lifetime. The earliest prayer, *subuh* ("soo-BUH"), is said from about 5:45 A.M. to 6 A.M. to coincide with the first blush of dawn. The *zuhur* ("zoo-HUR") hour is at noon, *asar* ("AH-sar") at 4 P.M., *mahgrib* ("MAH-grib") at dusk, and *isyak* ("EE-shah") after dark. Not every Muslim observes all the hours of prayer, but the call to prayer is heard from the towers of mosques. Sung by a gifted cantor in the old days, the prayers today are recordings, replayed and amplified.

Muslims wash their face, hands, and feet before prayer, and put on special clothes. Men wear long sleeves, long trousers, or a cotton *sarung* ("SAH-rohng"). They cover their heads with a rimless black hat called a *songkok* or, if they have performed the pilgrimage, a flat white cap. Women drape a voluminous garment around themselves to go to the mosque or when praying at home.

One month of the Muslim calendar is devoted to fasting, or *puasa* ("poo-ah-sah"). During this month, known as the Ramadan, no food or water may be consumed from before dawn until after dark. Night is turned into day with a "breakfast" after the evening prayer, a dinner at midnight, and a sustaining predawn meal before *subuh* prayers.

In the days of sailing ships, the pilgrimage to Mecca was a momentous undertaking. Not many men, and very few women, ever saw the holy places. Today the Malaysian government encourages Muslims to undertake the pilgrimage. Through a savings plan, people can accumulate the necessary funds. The Pilgrimage Board arranges the trip for them.

Mosques and *surau* are places of prayer and gathering. They are very plainly furnished. The congregation sits or kneels on the floor, each man on his own prayer rug. In a niche facing the Holy Land, there is a lectern and a bookstand holding the Koran. There are no holy pictures or statues inside a mosque or Muslim household, as holy images are strictly forbidden by Islam.

Celebrating Deepavali at a temple. There are many legends explaining the origins of the festival. One oft-told tale is how Lord Krishna killed the tyrannical King Naraka of Asura in answer to the prayers of his oppressed subjects.

HINDUISM

Hinduism is one of the oldest living religions, dating to prehistoric times in India. Hindus revere a pantheon of gods, led by the Lord Shiva, who rides on a bull, and his consort Durga, who is usually portrayed astride a tiger. The august couple symbolize creation, preservation, and destruction. The main feature of the Hindu religion is that there is no compulsion to do a certain thing. Pious Hindus have a little shrine in the house where lamps are lit and offerings of flowers and fruit are made daily, but no divine wrath threatens if this ritual is omitted. People go to the temple as and when it suits them, not because it is the holy day of the week.

By living a good life, Hindus can ensure that they will be reincarnated as a good person in their next life. A miscreant may be reborn as a low animal or an insect. Hindus sometimes consult an elaborate horoscope before making important decisions. A religious man interprets it for them.

Malaysian Indians celebrate a number of festivals, among them Deepavali. Deepavali is the Hindu festival of lights, symbolizing the triumph of good over evil. It is observed by Hindus of all sects. The family cleans the house and puts on their best clothes. They decorate the house and garden with candles and oil lamps that twinkle at dusk. Deepavali marks the end of the business year for some communities.

Chinese devotees holding joss sticks at a temple festival. Chinese temples hold figurines of various gods and often a Buddha as well.

TAOISM, CONFUCIANISM, AND BUDDHISM

Most Chinese in Malaysia would say simply that they are "Buddhists" or "Confucianists." The picturesque Chinese temples in the country house figurines of many different Chinese gods and often a statue of Buddha as well. However, these temples are not strictly Buddhist.

Buddhism and Confucianism are said to appeal to the intellect, while a popular version of Taoism is considered the religion of the masses. (Most Chinese engage in the practices of all three faiths.) Taoism venerates a multitude of gods. The gods and their adventures are easier to understand than details of Buddhist philosophy. Regional and local gods, deified heroes, and ancestors have a place in the Chinese temple. The Chinese who migrated to Malaysia over the centuries brought along their own gods and scholars. The village temple was often the site of the school, and the temple committee was also the school committee.

Temple festivals follow the Chinese lunar calendar. The beginning of the new moon is celebrated by lighting incense sticks (known as joss sticks) or burning "hell money" in big-bellied incinerators. "Hell money" is the term for banknotes of huge denominations (not real of course), sold for a few dollars per bundle, that humans use to pay celestial debts.

CHRISTIANITY

The first Christian churches in Malaysia were built in Melaka after 1511 by the Portuguese. In 1553, the remains of St. Francis Xavier were interred temporarily in the cathedral at Melaka until a permanent resting place was found in Goa in India.

The Portuguese cathedral suffered the fate of many pioneering religious edifices. When the Dutch took control of Melaka in 1641, they converted the cathedral to a Protestant church and renamed it St. Paul's Cathedral. The Dutch also added Christ Church to the town's landscape. This blood-red building, constructed in the Northern Renaissance style, can still be visited today.

Christian churches were constructed in Penang, too, and later in Singapore. These churches mostly served the foreign trading community. The Malay inhabitants of the peninsula remained Muslims.

In the early 19th century, there was considerable Christian missionary activity in Sarawak and North Borneo (Sabah). The missionaries usually left the Muslims on the peninsula alone and concentrated on the animist tribes. Today both Sabah and Sarawak have significant numbers of Christian Malaysians.

The present clergical members of the various churches in Malaysia are rarely foreigners. The bishops, priests, pastors, moderators, officers, and presidents of the Catholic, Anglican, and major Protestant churches in Malaysia are now mostly local.

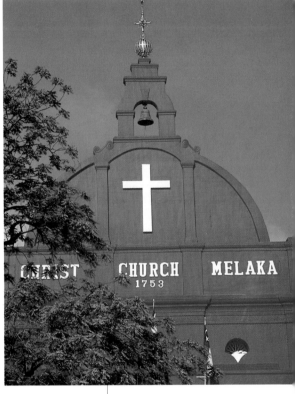

Christ Church in Melaka was built by the Dutch during their rule.

Iban (an East Malaysian tribe) hunters with blowpipes. Many Malaysians have embraced formal religions but still retain traces of old beliefs. The respect paid to rice in all its forms is a common animistic remnant.

ANIMISM

To an animist, all of nature is god. Most animists are jungle dwellers, exposed to climatic dangers and accidents that they hardly understand. Various spirits reside in various plants and animals. An insect calling from under the house may be a messenger from the underworld. A python crawling into an Orang Asli's jungle shelter may be the personification of a recently deceased family member and should therefore not be chased away. (Fortunately, the python is not a poisonous snake.) Each tree, each plant, each animal, and each sound has spiritual meaning, and the anger of any one of the many spirits brings bad luck.

Responsibility for bad luck is thus often conveniently shifted from man to the spirits. A farmer who hurts himself with his ax while felling trees is not careless or clumsy; he must have unknowingly offended one of the thousands of minor forest deities or forgotten some part of a taboo or ritual. His wound is just as painful, but the mishap is not directly his fault.

Animists in the Malay Peninsula and Borneo worship large trees, but their farming method forces them to clear parts of the jungle every year. They never fell a tree without first performing elaborate rituals to inform the wood spirits. An offering is placed on the stump of the first tree felled.

Some animist tribes never clear jungles, build houses, or do any form of communal work without first consulting the spirits of the jungle, which they believe are embodied in omen birds.

WHY THE IBAN OF SARAWAK LISTEN TO OMEN BIRDS

(as told by Manang Jabing of Rimbas)

"We Iban are not as ignorant as you may think. We, too, had writing once upon a time, but it was lost.

"Long, long ago there was a huge flood. All the world's people had to run and swim for it. The European put a page of his writing into his hat. The Chinese stuffed a sheet of his letters into the breast pocket of his shirt. But our ancestor had neither hat nor shirt, so he put his writing into the back of his loincloth and swam for his life.

"Later they met on high land. The European took the paper out of his hat. It was dry, and everybody could read it. The Chinese took the paper out of his pocket. It had got wet and the ink was running. That's why Chinese writing looks so squiggly and nobody else can read it.

"The Iban took his paper out of his waistband. It was wet too, so he spread it out on a low bush to dry. Then he went off to the jungle to look for a little hunting; the flood had made him hungry.

"When he came back to retrieve his writing, the sheet was gone. Birds had eaten it.

"The birds have eaten all our ancestors' wisdom. No wonder the birds are so wise. If we want to know when to start a farm, to build a house, to go hunting or fishing, we ask the birds. They've got the writing—they can tell us."

SUPERSTITIONS

Chinese-speaking Malaysians have many superstitions regarding numbers. Depending on the dialect and therefore the pronunciation, a number may mean something important or dreadful. For instance, the number eight sounds like "prosperity" in Mandarin and Cantonese, making August 8, 1988 (or 8–8–88) one of the luckiest days of the 20th century. Droves of couples married on that date, confident of conjugal bliss. It is too soon to say whether they all lived happily ever after!

September 9, 1999 was a similarly auspicious date for Malaysian couples. That day, nearly three times more couples registered to marry than usual.

For Hokkien speakers, the number four is pronounced like the word for death, *si*. Car owners are likely to object if their license plate contains such an unlucky digit. Picture the indignation of the Penang gentleman who was given the license plate number "PAK-4." Pronounced *pak si* ("pahk-SEE"), this roughly means, "Drop dead."

Many superstitions relate to birth and death. Pregnant women are not allowed to attend funerals, and they are carefully protected from ghosts and vampires.

"Prosper and grow, prosper and grow" is what the number on this car sounds like in Cantonese. The Chinese willingly pay premium prices for license plates like this one.

Few Malaysians go to a graveyard without good reason. The Chinese are known to visit graveyards in the dead of night bearing offerings in the hope of receiving lucky lottery numbers from dead relatives. A body kept in the house prior to burial is carefully watched—it is believed that if a cat happens to jump over the coffin, the corpse will become a ghoul!

Abandoned houses, dark trees, and tombs are thought to be haunted. The two rules of thumb regarding these are: keep away from such places or approach them and wrest a lucky omen from the resident ghost.

STRONG FOLK BELIEF IN MAGIC

When asked, most educated Malaysians insist they are not superstitious. Yet magicians, mediums, witch doctors, and faith healers of all kinds enjoy good business in Malaysia.

There is a general belief that while the (usually Western-trained) doctor at the local hospital may be a very good person, he or she can only deal with naturally caused sickness. Penicillin is not much use against an enemy's wicked spells. Only a spell more wicked than the original will deal with that sort of complaint. At times like that, a Malaysian will consult a *bomoh* ("boh-MOH").

The Malay magician, the *bomoh*, specializes in protective magic. Some states retain a *bomoh* to ensure good weather during open-air festivities.

Many *kampung* sports teams employ magic to help them win. A *bomoh* blows holy smoke over the team's football boots or equips them with amulets. If he can get to the field before the match (the home team will guard against such an occurrence), he plants a little charm near the goalposts.

Many children wear magic safeguards in the form of silver capsules, sacred threads, or rattan bracelets. A cross on a little chain is not just a symbol of the wearer's religion but a talisman to ward off evil. Non-Christians may sneak into a Catholic church to "borrow" some of the holy water there.

Some magicians perform black magic to inflict damage. Evil spirits are called to the magician's aid. A really bad magician tells an egg to undermine a certain person's health, slowly rot his flesh, and dissolve his very bones. The victim must find a more powerful *bomoh* to defuse the spell and send out a stronger one against the instigator. And so it goes, like the escalation of an arms race!

During the seventh month of the Chinese lunar calendar, the ghosts of all persons who have died unknown, unmourned, or unburied roam the earth. Offerings, joss sticks, hell money, and public entertainment mollify them and send them back to where they came from. Nicely treated, "hungry ghosts" give little trouble; nobody wants to know how they would act if they were neglected!

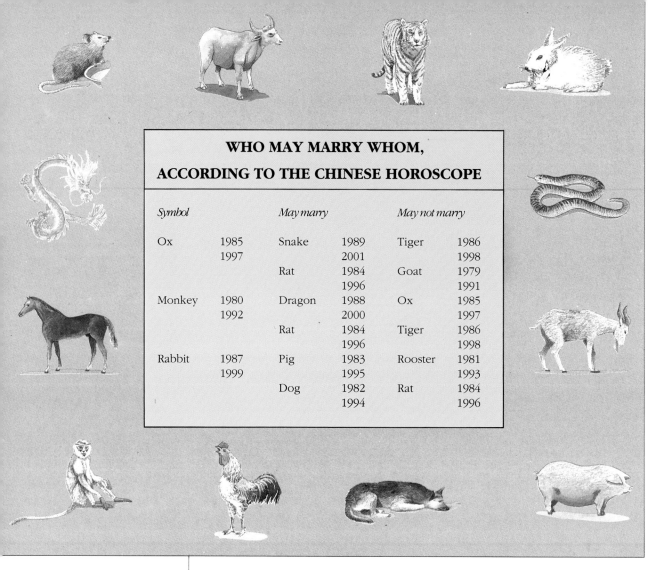

WHO MAY MARRY WHOM, ACCORDING TO THE CHINESE HOROSCOPE

Symbol		May marry		May not marry	
Ox	1985	Snake	1989	Tiger	1986
	1997		2001		1998
		Rat	1984	Goat	1979
			1996		1991
Monkey	1980	Dragon	1988	Ox	1985
	1992		2000		1997
		Rat	1984	Tiger	1986
			1996		1998
Rabbit	1987	Pig	1983	Rooster	1981
	1999		1995		1993
		Dog	1982	Rat	1984
			1994		1996

Chinese families are likely to consult horoscopes when a son or daughter is about to marry. Persons of some animal symbols are considered incompatible with some others.

ASTROLOGY AND SOOTHSAYING

The revelation that former U.S. President Ronald Reagan was interested in astrology may have shocked his own countrymen, but it did not ruffle any feathers in Southeast Asia where many statesmen have a personal astrologer. It is understood that a sensible man needs more than human guidance to make important decisions.

When a baby is born, especially the first son, Hindu families may ask an astrologer to cast a horoscope for the child's entire life. The very minute of the infant's birth has to be determined, and from there his life will be charted by the stars.

The Chinese zodiac has a 12-year cycle, with each year guarded by an animal, such as a pig, rabbit, or tiger. Each animal represents certain personality traits, and a person born in the year of that animal is believed to assume some of the animal's traits.

Malaysians generally like to peer into the future by means other than horoscopes too. One can consult a professional fortuneteller, who may have a name plate outside his door reading *Tukang Ramal* ("too-KANG RAH-mahl"), meaning "future maker." He uses various methods; palm reading is fairly widespread, but is not the only technique.

Some fortunetellers keep a tame animal such as a mouse or hamster. Strips of paper are put into its cage for it to tear into shreds. The client's fortune is then predicted from the scraps that fall outside the cage.

Many fortunetellers set up shop on the roadside or on covered walkways outside shophouses.

Many Chinese temples employ mediums who can work themselves into a trance and tell fortunes by uttering cryptic remarks that must be interpreted by a competent attendant.

The do-it-yourself method is to borrow a bamboo quiver full of long wooden or ivory sticks from the temple guardian. The devotee, having offered prayers, incense, and suitable gifts, shakes the quiver until one or several sticks fall out. The future is deciphered by interpreting the inscriptions on the various sticks.

Unlike their counterparts at carnivals in the West, fortunetellers and astrologers are respected members of the Malaysian community. While orthodox religions like Islam and Christianity are not entirely at ease with these practices, the general public patronizes astrologers in large numbers.

LANGUAGE

THE OFFICIAL LANGUAGE of Malaysia is Bahasa Malaysia, a standardized form of Malay. *Bahasa* ("bah-hah-sah") means language. Malay has long been the lingua franca of the Malay Archipelago. Natives and traders from Sumatra to the Philippines and those living in the coastal areas of Borneo and New Guinea can often speak some form of Malay.

MULTILINGUALISM

The official language is not the only language, of course. Chinese is spoken by Malaysia's second largest ethnic group: some 5.5 million Chinese. They may not understand one another, as the various Chinese dialects—Hakka, Cantonese, Hainanese, and Teochew—may be mutually unintelligible. A Malaysian Chinese may speak to another in a Chinese dialect, Malay, or even English.

Above: **While Bahasa Malaysia is the language of instruction in schools, some government-run schools teach a few classes a week in Chinese or Indian mother tongues.**

Opposite: **A newsstand selling magazines mostly in Bahasa Malaysia.**

The 1.5 million Indians in Malaysia are also divided into linguistic units: Tamil, Telugu, Punjabi, Hindi, Gujarati, and Urdu. East Malaysia is the land of the "small" languages—some used by just a few thousand people—because rugged terrain and intertribal warfare have isolated people from one another. Some Sarawak languages are Iban, Bidayuh, Melanau, Kayan, Kenyah, Kelabit, and Lun Dayeh. In Sabah one might hear Rungus, Murut, Bisaya, Bajau, Illanun, and Suluk.

NEWSPAPERS IN MALAYSIA

Not all Malaysians are literate, but those who are will spend some time each day reading the newspaper.

Newspapers in Malaysia come in a variety of languages, including

Bahasa Malaysia, English, a few Chinese and Indian languages, and Kadazan. The majority of these newspapers are printed in Roman script, but some languages have their own scripts.

Malay has no script of its own. Islamic missionaries brought with them the Koran and a system of writing that could be used to transcribe Malay quite accurately. The Arabic script, known as *jawi* ("jah-wee") in Malaysia, is still used for some religious and formal purposes.

When Europeans first began to travel and trade in the region, they recorded names and technical terms that interested them in a rough and ready fashion. Depending on whether the scribe was Portuguese, Dutch, or English, he would write "Suraia," "Soeraja," or "Sooraya" for the

Malaysian newsstands sell newspapers in several languages. In English, one can choose from *The New Straits Times*, *Star*, or *Malay Mail*; in Chinese, *Sin Chew Jit Poh* or *Nanyang Siang Pau*; in Malay, *Berita Harian* or *Utusan Melayu*; and in Tamil, *Tamil Nesan*, *Malaysia Nanbun*, or *Harian Thinamurassu*.

same name. Over the years, a generally accepted Romanized system of written Malay has crystallized. Malay newspapers are printed either in *jawi* or in Romanized Malay.

Chinese languages like Mandarin are written in ideograms. Each character stands for an idea or a combination of ideas. A "simplified" version of written Chinese—used in newspapers, among other things—contains 2,500 to 3,000 characters.

Indian language newspapers are printed in the specific scripts of Tamil, Punjabi, Urdu, and Malayalam. However, these languages can be rendered in Roman script for other purposes.

BAHASA MALAYSIA

Bahasa Malaysia is, in a way, a synthetic language. It is a standardized form of the dialect variants of the Malay language. Schoolchildren occasionally have difficulty distinguishing between "proper" language and the form they speak at home. The two are nearly the same, but not quite. Some non-Malays speak an imperfect form of Bahasa Malaysia called Bahasa Pasar ("pah-sahr"), which literally means language of the marketplace.

People of the various regions speak dialects of their own. Some dialects vary in stress patterns and speech rhythms; others in vocabulary. A Malay farmer from Johor would have to listen very carefully to understand what another Malay farmer from Terengganu is telling him. Both would find what a Malay colleague from Sabah tries to contribute to the conversation incomprehensible—yet all three speak Malay.

On television, when a non-Malay language program is shown, it is invariably accompanied by Malay subtitles.

Standard Bahasa Malaysia is the language heard on radio and television and taught in schools. Non-Malay language programs shown on Malaysian television channels often have Malay subtitles. The spelling of words in Bahasa Malaysia has been standardized to make the language more or less compatible with Bahasa Indonesia, a form of Malay spoken by about 100 million Indonesians.

The vocabulary is also being standardized and constantly revised. An educated Indonesian can understand an educated Malaysian, despite a few minor differences between their versions of the Malay language. These differences are not unlike those in the spoken English dialects and vocabularies of Americans, Canadians, and Britons.

SPEAK MALAY

Here are a few simple phrases in Bahasa Malaysia that you can try. Pronounce the vowels as follows: *a* as in "father," *e* as in "pet," *i* as in "pit," *o* as in "pot," and *u* as in "put."

Good morning!
Selamat pagi!

How are you?
Apa khabar?

Fine, thank you.
Baik, terima kasih.

What's your name?
Siapa nama anda?

My name is Ben.
Nama saya Ben.

Malaysia is hot, but it rains a lot.
Negeri Malaysia panas tetapi selalu hujan.

Come follow me!
Mari ikut saya!

My father's house is not very big.
Rumah ayah saya tidak berapa besar.

Come up the stairs to the house!
Sila naik tangga ke rumah!

Only my little sister is home; my parents are at work.
Hanya adik saya berada di rumah; ibu dan ayah saya sedang bekerja.

Please take off your shoes; it is our custom.
Sila buka kasut anda; inilah adat resam kami.

Have a seat, and I'll bring you a cool drink.
Sila duduk, dan saya akan membawa anda minuman segar.

BODY LANGUAGE

Verbal language is not all there is to communication. Body language sometimes does the trick. A shake of the head says "no" in most parts of the world, while a nod signifies agreement or acceptance. In Malaysia, some gestures are peculiar to an ethnic group, while some are common to all. For instance, it is generally not considered polite to point at persons or things with the index finger. A bent index finger or thumb is used to point—or rather to knuckle—in the right direction.

Malaysians do not touch each other unless they are close friends or relatives. In a crowd, a woman holds her dress to herself to avoid touching passersby with it.

Muslims greet one another by touching the other person's right hand and then their own chests. This is the *salam*, a gesture meaning "I greet you from my heart." It may be done with both hands to show greater deference, especially with older people.

Muslims greet each other by just touching the other's right hand and then their own chests. Conservative Muslim women will not shake hands with a man, but bow gently. The old-fashioned Chinese way of greeting—shaking hands at waist level while bowing—is used only by the older Chinese these days.

Similarly the Indian palm-to-palm greeting, *namaskar* ("neh-mehs-kehr"), is now used only at ceremonial occasions. Sikh men prefer to greet friends with a heavy pat on the back, a pummelling sort of welcome. The Western handshake is increasingly being used as a form of greeting, especially in the business community.

In courtship, the language of sighs and glances is used: a young lady's seemingly innocent offer of a quid of betel* to a young man, or a lace handkerchief dropped where he is sure to find it, speaks volumes.

* Parings of betel nut with a dash of lime paste are wrapped in a betel leaf and then chewed for enjoyment.

A *pantun* contest held by the national television station.

CONTEST OF WORDS

Malaysians respect an articulate, confident speaker. A child's early training in reciting the Koran before an audience is often given as an example of early preparation for public speech.

A traditional form of entertainment at parties is the *pantun* ("pahn-toon"). Originally a Malay pastime, it has become familiar to other Malaysians, especially the Straits Chinese. The men compose humorous quatrains to challenge the women. One of the women answers, usually with the necessary sting. Another man speaks up for his gender, and another woman rebuts. This merry exchange goes on until dawn and is by no means confined to the young. You do not learn to improvise well until you have seen a few birthdays!

A *pantun* can also express tender sentiment, but recited in front of a festive crowd, the message is veiled.

Kalau tuan mudik ke hulu
Carikan sahaja bunga kemoja
Kalau tuan mati dahulu
Nantikan sahaja di pintu syurga.

Should you travel upstream
Find me a sweet-scented flower
Should you die before I do
Wait for me at heaven's gates.

THE BROADCAST MEDIA

Broadcasting only began in Peninsular Malaysia in 1946 and in East Malaysia in the 1950s. Television was introduced in 1963 and extended to East Malaysia in 1972. Most programs are in Bahasa Malaysia, with air time also provided for programs in English (mainly from the United States), Chinese and Indian dialects, and East Malaysian regional languages. States have their own radio studios.

There are four free-to-air television channels: the state-run Radio Television Malaysia TV1 and TV2 and the privately owned TV3 launched in the mid-1980s and NTV7 launched in 1998. Television advertising has done a lot to mold the tastes and ideas of Malaysia's young people. However remote a village, so long as there is electricity, there will be at least one television set displaying the tastes and habits of the middle class to a dazzled rural audience. Most young Malaysians long to get to a big town to see the glamour promised by the consumption-oriented media.

A musical gala, organized jointly by Malaysia's RTM and TV Indonesia and aired live in both countries.

Oral tradition wilts before the onslaught of electronic sound. Excellent cultural programs show the best traditional performers. The immediate reaction of a *kampung*-renowned specialist is: "This is a lot better than I can do. I should lose face if I sang this song again!" The prospective audience probably will not urge the village star to perform his act anyway. They are too busy watching television!

In remote areas, the radio may be the community's only immediate link with the outside world. Forty-five news bulletins are broadcast daily from the national station. Regional stations repeat them in local dialects.

ARTS

DRAMA IN MALAYSIA is the product of foreign influence. The best-known dramatic arts in Malaysia are imports: *wayang kulit* and *bangsawan* from Indonesia and Chinese opera from China.

Making up for the absence of traditional local drama is an impressive body of original Malaysian literature. Some of it was first written in the 19th century, based on oral sources. Some, especially East Malaysian tribal literature, remains unrecorded to this day.

TRADITIONAL LITERATURE

Sagas in which fact and legend blend are known in every state. The stirring tales of Admiral Hang Tuah and his noble fellows are still enjoyed by listeners and readers alike. The history of Malaya has been recorded in *Sejarah Melayu*, the Malay Annals. The narrative starts with Alexander the Great, who is described as the ancestor of Malay royalty. As the story gets to the 14th or 15th century, it becomes a verifiable historical record. If the doings of the 16th-century sultans are not uniformly edifying, they are certainly interesting.

The works of a 19th-century Malay author, Munshi Abdullah, are still studied in schools as literature texts. A much-traveled and well-educated man, Abdullah wrote several books of travels as well as a story of Malay feudal and social history, *Kesah Pelayaran Abdullah* (Tales from Abdullah's Travel).

Malaysia also has its own version of Aesop's Fables, the most popular being *Hikayat Sang Kanchil*. This is a collection of tales revolving around the adventures of a little mousedeer as it outwits larger and stronger animals and human beings. There is a moral to be learned from each tale, and every Malaysian child knows a story from the entertaining *Hikayat Sang Kanchil*.

Above: **There are many tales of heroism about the legendary Admiral Hang Tuah of the Melaka Sultanate. But there is one that especially delights audiences—how he stole a bride for Sultan Mansur Shah. The lady in question was betrothed to a man she did not love. Hang Tuah charmed her so that she fell in love with him and willingly fled with him to Melaka. On the way, Hang Tuah broke the charm so that she fell in love with the sultan.**

Opposite: **Rebana ubi drummers of Kelantan. On festive occasions the drummers compete to see who can keep the beat going the longest.**

DANCE

Traditional dances are popular, but few Malaysians learn them thoroughly. Schoolgirls usually learn the basic movements of a Malay dance called Bunga Melor or learn dances set to Chinese tunes.

Those who want to dance seriously face hard training, like the Western ballerina. Stress is laid on supple hands—a classical Malay dancer can bend her fingers back to almost touch her forearm!

To first-timers, East Malaysian dance looks torturous. Parties fill a longhouse with guests almost to bursting point. A dance of vigorous leaps and bounds might just prove too much for the building!

MAK YONG Mak Yong is a dance from Kelantan set to traditional Malay music. The violin whines the tune, while studded gongs and skin drums throb a rhythm of mesmerizing monotony.

After the stage has been cleaned, gorgeously costumed dancers enter. The male lead, Pak Yong, is good-looking to the point of being pretty—for good reason: "he" is danced by a girl, as are all the male characters except one aged clown.

Mak Yong used to be organized to amuse the sultan's women in the court. Handsome young men could not perform in the harem! The clown was old enough to be "trustworthy" and many of his lines are ribald references to this fact.

EAST MALAYSIAN DANCES East Malaysians have preserved many of their people's traditional dances. Dayak children, for example, learn to dance at an early age. The slow but complicated movements of their traditional dances require excellent muscle control. Dancing is supposed to make boys agile and girls graceful.

MALAY DANCE Some old Malay dances have been adapted to modern use. Ronggeng and joget, traditionally danced by men only before an audience, are performed as "mixed doubles" on the dance floor nowadays. The decencies must be preserved, of course—throughout the fairly intricate gyrations of a ronggeng, the couple never touch. Their bodies and arms make reciprocal movements, hands almost but never quite meet. A traditional courtly dance is the Joget Gamelan. It is danced to the sounds of the xylophone, gong, and drums. The graceful dancers don elaborate costumes complete with a headdress, a silk blouse, and a long silk scarf. To foreign eyes the classical Malay dances have something of a Spanish air, partly because of their common Moorish heritage.

INDIAN DANCE An Indian girl who wants to learn her people's classical dances is advised to start by age 5. There are teachers who are prepared to take a student through her early steps, not forgetting initiation prayers before the Lord Shiva, god of dance, at whose altar she must present her jingling anklets.

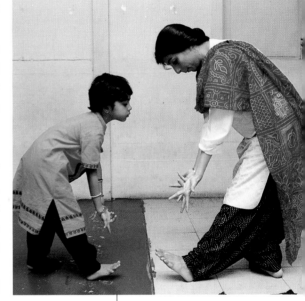

An Indian teacher taking her young novice through her paces.

Basic classical dancing involves about 100 steps and movements, which are choreographed into dance dramas of old narratives. When the novice reaches her 10th or 11th year, she is ready to perform solo the six major dances of the Bharathanatyam, the 16th-century Indian classical dance.

After this display, which is an examination at the same time, the girl will be able to take her place among the mature dancers in temple ceremonies and public performances.

MUSIC OF THE MALAY PENINSULA

The original music of the Malay Peninsula is percussive. Long ago, large gongs served to send messages from one place to another. They still give the basic beat for many dances. Whole ensembles of gongs, from huge boomers to delicate tinklers, are used in the Javanese gamelan orchestra, which is occasionally heard in Malaysia too.

A Malay gong orchestra.

Besides gongs there are drums. The man-sized "long drums" of the northern part of the Malay Peninsula are made of hollowed out tree trunks, the ends of which are covered with taut buffalo or goat skin. Small tambourines are an import from the Arab world. They are beaten to the rhythm of the strident singing of Arab songs at many Malay weddings. The Arabs also brought a type of lute with them, the gambus, which is skillfully played by many Malays.

In many villages there is a *keroncong* ("kehr-rohng-chohng") band, an ensemble playing old-fashioned music on fiddles, hand-drums, small harmonicas, and sometimes flutes.

Peculiar to the courts of Kedah, Perak, Terengganu, and Selangor is the *nobat* ("noh-baht"), a band that consists of a straight, valveless silver trumpet, a flute, a gong, and a consort of drums. The *nobat* only performs on ceremonious royal occasions, such as a ruler's accession, wedding, or funeral. The music has a haunting quality. Few who have heard it once can forget the *nobat*.

Malaysia's indigenous peoples, the Orang Asli, have their own brand of tribal music, the sounds of which originate from natural materials like gourd, cane, wood, and bamboo.

EAST MALAYSIAN MUSIC

In the past, among the people of Sabah and Sarawak, gongs were considered more than musical instruments. Brought into the country by barter trade, they were symbols of wealth and stability as well. Many old rituals involve the use of gongs. The Bidayuh wash their ancestral head trophies in an overturned gong filled with coconut water. Iban bridal couples sit on a pair of gongs.

Many reed and bamboo flutes are used in East Malaysia. Some, those

A bamboo bass flute.

that resemble the jew's harp, produce a sound so soft it can only be heard by someone near the performer. Others are used at ceremonies and parties and can be quite shrill. Flute tunes are usually brief motifs of arpeggios, repeated over and over again with minor variations. It is not common for people to sing when wind instruments are being played. Natives of Borneo also play a mouth-organ that has bamboo pipes that stand up and a gourd that serves as a wind chamber.

A string instrument native to Sabah is the *jotong utong* (bamboo zither). A thick piece of bamboo has strips of its skin lifted up; each section is pegged with little wedges to stretch and tune it.

The wood xylophone consists of hardwood sticks of varying lengths stretched on a string ladder.

The *jotong utong* (bamboo zither).

The sape is a string instrument played by the Kenyah and Kayan of central Borneo. It is made out of a single piece of wood and has two to four strings. Expert players rearrange the frets for happy and solemn tunes.

Brass bands add to the pomp and pageantry of the National Day Parade on August 31.

MODERN MUSIC

Much Malaysian patriotic music would sound sentimental to the foreign ear. Love for the nation is expressed in the same swooning tones and words that are used in love songs, often in tunes strongly reminiscent of Indonesian *keroncong*.

On big occasions and at rallies, processions, and open-air functions, sentiment gives way to big drums and brass bands. They can rival the best when it comes to oom-pah-pah. Military units, the police, schools, and even private firms maintain brass bands of varying quality.

As for modern music, you name it, Malaysia has it. Besides obvious copycat efforts like the Malaysian Elvis Presley, there are excellent indigenous modern bands.

Musical preferences can lead to tense situations among *kampung* youngsters if one village likes heavy metal and the next prefers rock. Nearly every village has its own band, a couple of electric guitars, and the required amount of percussion. The amplifiers are always in great shape if nothing else is. In the bigger towns, there are modern dance bands with an ever-changing supply of performers and singers. Malaysia has many talented musicians. Each year a few make it to the top.

Batik, the traditional method of wax-resistant fabric printing, has become an accepted artistic medium.

VISUAL ART

Malaysia shares with Indonesia the tradition of *batik*, wax-resistant fabric printing used in cloth production. In recent years, however, *batik* has also become an accepted artistic medium.

Young painters have branched off from the traditional, Dutch-inspired style used by old masters like Mohammad Hoessein bin Enas, a well-known portrait painter who uses mainly oils. Young painters experiment with abstract renditions of their ideas in modern media like tempera, acrylic, and collage.

There are many art clubs throughout Malaysia. Members get together for sketching and study sessions and go for occasional working trips outdoors. Visitors to a popular picnic spot are used to the sight of half a dozen artists perched on as many boulders in the middle of a rushing rapid, serenely sketching on folios balanced on their knees. Nothing but a heavy shower will drive them away from their vantage points!

Chinese brush painting is an art form brought to Malaysia by immigrants, that is now well-established. Besides traditional motifs, some painters depict local scenery, fruit, insects, and wildlife in the quick, fluid brush strokes typical of this style.

Dondang sayang, literally love song, is popular at weddings and other celebrations, particularly among the people of Melaka. A male and a female singer, accompanied by drums, gongs, and violins, exchange witty *pantuns* to the delight of the audience. This can go on for hours.

PUBLIC SPEAKING AS AN ART

Malaysians of all races value an articulate speaker who can stand up and say his piece on any occasion. There is a body of traditional literature that was only preserved orally until the quite recent past. Some of it is still unrecorded and in danger of being lost.

The traditional pastimes survive to a limited extent in the *kampung* and longhouses of remote areas. They are also enjoying a new lease of life as public entertainment. At official and private functions, it is considered chic to have a recitation of an excerpt of one of the interminable *syair* ("shaheer") stories or a Mak Yong performance.

Schools organize rhetoric and speech contests to encourage students to speak confidently and freely. Rhetoric tends to degenerate into ranting in some cases, but the standard of debating is usually quite high. Interschool debates are "fought" by proper rules in general, with regional variants. However, a speaker will lose points for pointing at the opposing side. This is not against Western debating etiquette but is definitely bad manners in Malaysia.

HANDICRAFTS

On the eastern coast of Peninsular Malaysia, fishing is a main source of income. People still have the leisure to embellish their boats, which are necessities of life in a very real sense. This adds a splash of color to the typical scene of a long white beach bordered by deep green jungle and dark green sea.

In Sarawak, Borneo's best backstrap loom weavers are to be found. Iban women tie-dye the warp threads of their cotton fabric into intricate traditional patterns. When the cloth is woven, the ready-made patterns appear. Many Malaysian men are woodcarvers who like to beautify articles of daily use with fretwork, whittling, or surface incision. The fascia boards of old-fashioned Malay houses are often thus decorated, as are women's weaving utensils, game boards, headboards, and mirror frames.

Above: **Kite fighting is a sport; kite making an art. This old gentleman has a lifetime's experience behind him when it comes to cutting, pasting, stringing, and properly balancing the frail craft. He paints and decorates it to rival the other villages' best in kite competitions.**

Left: **Carving a tall ceremonial post to be erected next to a long-house.**

LEISURE

Many of Malaysia's popular pastimes involve some form of competition. Besides the likes of hopscotch and jacks, children play "scissors, paper, stone" called *kuncum* ("koon-choom"). On the count of *kuncum,* each player makes a hand symbol: two pointed fingers for scissors, an open palm for paper, or a clenched fist for stone. Who wins depends on the combination of symbols. The scissors cuts the paper, the stone breaks the scissors, and the paper wraps the stone.

Even kites compete in Malaysia. The kite line is dipped in glue and then in powdered glass so it will cut an opponent's line if skillfully flown. Playing out line is so hazardous that many "kite fighters" wear one leather glove. Kite-flying competitions are held among villages. The champions are grown men.

Spinning tops can be used for fighting, as can quoits, somewhat like pitching horseshoes. An elaborate version of coconut shy involves throwing half a coconut shell over prizes. If the shell covers an item, the contestant can claim it.

Schoolboys have fighting fish in jars and fighting beetles in match boxes. Their elder brothers play a more exciting game that strikes most foreigners as cruel: cockfighting, even though it is illegal in Malaysia.

Opposite: **A young boy learning the traditional Malay art of kite-making from his grandfather.**

MAHJONG

Played extensively by the Chinese community in Malaysia, *mahjong* is usually played by four persons who use 136 or 144 plastic tiles, depending on which rules are being used. *Mahjong* is very similar to the card game gin rummy. The object of the game is to be the first to obtain a complete set of tiles. *Mahjong* tiles are intricately carved with pictures of flowers, Chinese characters, and bamboo.

FISHING

Some Malaysians make their living as fishermen. Others wish they could earn enough from fishing to suit their lifestyle—this, at any rate, explains Malaysians' abiding love for fish and fishing. Almost every settlement is near a river or the sea. The boat jetty or harbor wall is sure to be populated with men and boys using a variety of tackle. Urban wage-earners make weekend trips to promising spots such as waterfalls, rapids, a quiet bridge, or an old embankment that promises undisturbed communion with the fish.

Holiday "chalets" on stilts. The sun, sea, and fresh air more than make up for the spartan facilities.

Many people like to stretch nets across little rivers or to set traps. A common fish trap looks like a long round basket, with an entry hole defended by tapering rattan rods. A fish can get in but not out. The owner of the trap opens a little hinged door in the side of the basket to collect his catch.

Malaysians' well-known love for water and fishing has led to a small industry providing accommodation in modest seaside and riverside huts or elegantly styled "chalets" that are rented out by the day or week. Such shelters are usually very basic, with a sleeping room, a cooking facility, and some sort of washroom. The rent is paid for the whole unit; the owner does not care how many people are jammed into it for a few days. Families, school classes, clubs—any group that cannot afford to stay at a proper "beach resort"—get all the fun of beach, river, or island entertainment at a modest price.

WATER SPORTS

There are many beach resorts in Malaysia, and very elegant ones at that. Hotels and clubs on the wide beaches of the eastern coast of Peninsular Malaysia and Borneo invite the affluent vacationer to a sunny stay filled with windsurfing, snorkeling, scuba diving, sailing, or simply lounging on the warm sand. Malaysian beach resorts have become so popular with tourists that Club Med recently built one of its resorts on the eastern coast of the peninsula.

Food at such establishments is usually of the international hotel-cuisine type, heavy on seafood. Some guests have their own catch cooked for dinner. Knowledgeable tourists, however, wander beyond their hotel. There is sure to be a *kampung* or a bazaar nearby. The same lobster, garoupa, turtle eggs, or crab found in the hotel is sizzled up here in full view of the hungry consumer, spiced with whatever the regional flavor dictates, and sold at a fraction of the price it would go for in a hotel.

Malaysia has the natural advantage of a tropical climate. Occasionally it can be too windy or too rainy for outdoor sports, but it is never too cold. Even during the rainy season, some fine days can be enjoyed by water sports enthusiasts and beach lovers.

Scuba diving off the eastern state of Terengganu.

Malaysia's larger towns have their own water sports clubs and facilities. Scuba diving is a new sport fast catching on among affluent Malaysians. Even in the *kampung*, boys may be seen equipped with snorkels, flippers, and diving goggles and chasing the sea and river fish with their bamboo fishing spears.

LAND SPORTS

BALL GAMES Soccer and cricket caught on like wildfire in the Malaya of the early 20th century. Basketball, table tennis, and badminton are popular in present-day Malaysia.

There is also a local sport, somewhat resembling volleyball, called *sepak takraw* ("say-pahk tahk-raw"). It means "hit the ball."

Originating in the courts of Siam (Thailand) and Melaka, the game used to involve two or more players who formed a circle and kicked, shouldered, and headed a hollow rattan ball to one another. The object was to keep the ball from touching the ground. *Kampung* boys still play it this way. Exact rules were drawn up in 1946, and a net, as well as a proper scoring system, was introduced. The game was formally included in the Southeast Asia Games in 1965, played by teams from Malaysia, Brunei, Indonesia, Thailand, Burma, Singapore, and the Philippines.

A *sepak takraw* team consists of two wings and one back, the *tekong* ("teh-kohng"), who opens the game by kicking the ball across the net. Unlike volleyball, each player can hit the ball three times in succession. The ball may be hit with any part of the body other than the hands or arms, which serve mainly as wings to balance the players' acrobatic leaps and tumbles.

MARTIAL ARTS Silat is an old Malay form of self-defense, not unlike shadowboxing. Small boys are taught the basic movements, unarmed. Mock fighting is not encouraged by silat masters until the combatants have learned discipline and restraint.

In urban areas, other forms of self-defense are popular. Many join taekwondo classes, kicking their feet over their heads with great gusto.

Older people are sometimes seen in the town parks, in the cool of dawn, practicing slow, rhythmic movements called t'ai chi. This very ancient Chinese martial art, now much prized as a form of exercise, is believed to strengthen the body without exhausting or overstraining it.

MALAYSIANS AND MUSIC

There is usually a band of boys and girls in a Malay *kampung* who beat goatskin tambourines, accompanied by the drummers' own singing. A good band can be in demand for weddings and other festive occasions throughout the district.

Chinese music enthusiasts get together to form chamber groups. These dispense with the percussion that gives Chinese opera its deafening resonance, using knee-fiddles, flutes, lutes, and sometimes one softly played tambourine.

In the towns, formal Western music lessons are available, and many middle-class children are encouraged to learn to play the piano. Most of them drop out of their piano lessons after a few years, but the few talented performers reach admirable standards. Malaysian music students take British examinations from the Royal School of Music or Trinity College.

Malaysians who do not play a musical instrument, sing. Schoolchildren sing; fishermen sing; soldiers sing; even birds' nests collectors sing on the way to their dangerous work in deep caves. Many Malaysians are members of church or secular choirs. Office staff choirs serenade visitors. School choirs are inevitable. Malaysian teenagers often go through a feverish stage of trying to imitate successful U.S. pop stars like Michael Jackson, M.C. Hammer, and even Madonna!

DRAMATIC PURSUITS

Malaysia does not have any indigenous drama. People are fond of watching dramatic performances, but not until quite recently did it become acceptable for respectable citizens or their children to be seen on stage. Instead "outsiders" used to entertain Malaysian audiences.

The *bangsawan*, once a traveling show, was something like an operetta. The involved plot was broken by unconnected interludes called "extra turns" that permitted one actor to garner a little separate applause and maybe a shower of coins. Stories and music were often improvised by the performers. One *bangsawan* popular before the war was called "Lohengrin and His Big Duck"—Wagner's grand opera adapted

A *wayang kulit* show. The shadows on the screen usually tell a story from the Hindu epics— the Mahabharata and the Ramayana.

to suit a culture where swans were unknown!

Many *bangsawan* performers were children, who were bought from their parents or shadier sources for this trade. The court books of the prewar period are full of complaints against *bangsawan* masters ill-using their charges or even kidnapping pretty children before the show moved on to another town!

The famous Indonesian shadow play, *wayang kulit*, has been adopted by Malaysian performers. Puppets cut out of stiff leather are manipulated with a set of movable sticks behind a white sheet illuminated by a couple of kerosene lanterns.

Today's performers in Chinese opera are often amateurs. There is not enough demand for this entertainment to maintain professional singers and actors. Enthusiasts give up many hours of their free time to practice singing, master intricate stage movements and gestures, and manage cumbersome costumes.

Chinese opera—called *wayang* ("wah-young")—is a form of drama with close religious connections. A temple deity's birthday is often celebrated with an opera. The hungry ghosts that are believed to roam the land during the Chinese seventh month are generally appeased with lavish operatic performances. Quite young actors may get their early training in silent parts, as attendants or messengers, before graduating to prince, emperor, general, princess, or queen. While the roles of the emperor or the general are always sung by men, the part of the prince, especially in a romantic work, may be performed by a young woman. The part requires a very high tenor voice, and the character is supposed to look "sweet."

One ancient Malaysian spectator art is storytelling. Especially in the days when hardly anyone could read, before radio and television provided evening entertainment, a practiced storyteller could be sure of an enthralled audience. There is a Malay method of chanting a historical tale, called *syair,* which regularly entertained choice gatherings at royal parties.

One Sarawak story takes nine nights to tell. Longhouse festivals may involve three or four reciters who walk up and down the long veranda for up to eight hours without once stopping before their story-song is done!

AFTER SCHOOL

One very popular form of entertainment, especially for school-age youngsters, is wandering around shopping malls. Such expeditions are always undertaken in groups. A bunch of boys here and a bunch of girls there are fully aware of each other. They may very possibly follow each other around, even sit at adjoining tables in the hamburger joint, but no boy would say he had been "out with the girls."

Shopping itself is a secondary consideration to mall-walking. The main thing is meeting friends, gawking at strangers, and giggling at the local "freak show" provided by the occasional eccentric or unusually fashionable outfit or hairstyle.

If someone in the group is carrying a boom box, it is turned on to the maximum volume, regardless of what the shops are already producing by way of decibels.

Movie theaters are popular entertainment spots, as are skating rinks and bowling alleys, all to be visited by a group. One person arriving alone would feel out of place.

Boys who have them love to ride their motorcycles around town, slow enough for their friends to see, but fast enough to produce noise. After dark, there are illegal motorcycle races on the less frequented roads.

GOLD RUSH SYNDROME

Malaysians are a gregarious lot; they love to be wherever something is happening. A seemingly innocent notice in a newspaper or a rumor spread by word of mouth can spark off a mass movement. Queues may snake towards a spring said to have incredible healing powers. A miracle healer may attract a sudden influx of patients to a roadless village. A report on the sighting of a supernatural phenomenon in a lake or river or on a beach will draw crowds of sightseers. Once a stampede begins, there is no way to stop it except to let it die a natural death. In any case, everyone has a good time whether or not the object of curiosity shows up.

Once in a while, a small gold rush breaks out in Malaysia. A farmer finds gold dust or what he considers to be raw diamonds in his field. Within days, the place will be swarming with prospectors, each armed with a large flat pan called a *dulang* ("doo-lahng"), used for washing soil to extract the precious mineral. The gold may prove scanty or entirely absent, and the village will return to normal in good time.

The scene of a crime becomes a "sightseeing spot" for the ghoulish members of the public to the annoyance of the police who are investigating. Gawkers may block the fire engine from reaching a blaze. But then Malaysians are not unique in that respect.

Zoos, parks, and waterfronts are thronged with family groups on a Sunday, as are historical places and the more accessible picnic spots, including the Kota Tinggi waterfalls in Johor.

FESTIVALS

In the course of a year, Malaysians enjoy numerous public holidays to celebrate the religions and major festivals of the three main races—the Malays, Chinese, and Indians. Even if a Malaysian does not belong to the religion or culture that celebrates a particular festival, he or she will visit friends who do.

ANNUAL FESTIVALS

January/February	Chinese New Year
	Chap Goh Mei (Chinese)
	Thaiponggal (Hindu)
	Thaipusam (Hindu)
March/April	Good Friday (Christian)
May	Vesak Day (Buddhist)
May 30–31	Kadazan Harvest Festival (Kadazan)
June 1–2	Gawai Dayak (Sarawak natives)
August 31	National Day
October/November	Deepavali (Hindu)
December 25	Christmas (Christian)

The dates of the Islamic festivals—Hari Raya Puasa, Hari Raya Haji, Ma'al Hijrah, and Prophet Mohammed's birthday—follow the Islamic lunar calendar and can fall in a different month from one year to the next.

The dates of the Hindu and Buddhist festivals follow the Indian and Chinese lunar calendars and change from year to year, though not as drastically as the Islamic festival dates.

Opposite: **National Day (August 31) in Malaysia means a parade with uniforms, flags, and music. It is always a school holiday, but no schoolchild would dream of staying at home. National Day marks the date the Federation of Malaya and the former British colonies of Singapore, Sarawak, and Sabah united into the new nation of Malaysia. Singapore left the federation in 1965 but remains a good friend and neighbor.**

From the second to the 15th day of the Chinese New Year, acrobatic troupes bearing a pair of majestic lion heads are invited into shops and homes to bless the premises. Manned by two dancers, each lion moves to the beat of gongs and drums. In and out of the rooms, up and down the stairs, it finally comes to the family altar and bows to the ancestor tablets. The lion troupe receives an *ang pow* ("ahng-pow"), a red packet containing money, as a reward.

CHINESE NEW YEAR

Celebrating the new year is a bit of a problem in Malaysia. Which new year do you mean? There is the "ordinary" or "Western" New Year on Jan 1, the Chinese New Year, the Muslim New Year, and the Hindu New Year. Each is celebrated by some Malaysians, though the Chinese New Year must take the prize for noise and hilarity.

The Chinese New Year marks the beginning of a new lunar year; thus it falls on a different date each year. It can be as early as December or as late as March, though it usually falls in January or February.

In old times, the New Year was about the only holiday the lower classes had. To this day, stores shut for several days and businesses come to a standstill, while boss and worker hold family reunions, enjoy huge feasts, gamble a little "for luck" (unless they lose), and visit relatives and friends.

At midnight, some parts of the large towns burst into a cacophony of firecrackers. Firecrackers are officially banned in Malaysia, but some traditional Chinese families ignore the ban, as firecrackers are supposed to drive out evil spirits. They are also great entertainment. A middle-class family is likely to spend $40 to $190 on firecrackers.

On New Year's Day, when visitors come to each open house, the boys are likely to fire off a volley of firecrackers each time a particularly respected guest makes his way up the garden path. By the second or third day supplies are mercifully exhausted.

CHAP GOH MEI

Celebrated on the 15th day after the Chinese New Year, on the night of a full-moon, Chap Goh Mei fulfills the function that Twelfth Night does after Christmas: it marks the official end of the festivities.

Modern-day Chap Goh Mei is usually celebrated with a big family dinner. Many Chinese hang out red lanterns or switch on electric "fairy lights," and children let off the remnants of the firecrackers bought for the Chinese New Year.

At temples, a troupe of mediums may give displays of firewalking. Under the protection of a deity, the participants run or walk barefooted on burning coals in a pit 10 feet (3 m) long. Some mediums may lie down on the bed of coals unscorched and let the others walk over them.

In the old days, unmarried girls were taken to the waterfront on Chap Goh Mei to throw oranges into the river or sea and wish for a good husband. The young men of the town, dressed up and hair gleaming with oil, would be at the quays before the ladies arrived in their rickshaws. The young singles would flirt cautiously, since there was at least one chaperone in each rickshaw to look out for the young maidens.

Tamil Hindu farmers make rice offerings on Thaiponggal to thank the gods for a good harvest. While not many Tamil Hindus in Malaysia are farmers, Thaiponggal is still a major celebration. At dawn, vegetarian foods are presented to the gods, and a display of fruit and flowers is assembled, so that children see a vision of beauty first thing in the morning.

THAIPONGGAL

Thaiponggal is a harvest festival, celebrated unseasonably in January, because it is fixed on the Hindu calendar. Farmers rise while it is still dark and cook some of the newly harvested grain to present it to the sun at dawn. This is the ponggal.

Some urban families have adapted this ritual to their living conditions. The family rises, bathes, and gets dressed before dawn, without using any light. When all are ready in their best clothes, they assemble around a display of fruit and flowers. Lamps are lit. The first sight in the morning must be a vision of natural beauty. Dawn arrives, and a vegetarian breakfast is enjoyed by all.

THAIPUSAM

This festival is celebrated in the streets, with all the noise and excitement of a carnival. The day is consecrated to the Hindu deity Lord Subramaniam to celebrate his victory over evil forces and to fulfill vows made to him during the year.

Hindu devotees march in the streets in a long procession, carrying colorful displays of flowers and fruit. Libations of milk and honey are made in honor of the deity.

Helpers walk quietly alongside a *kavadi* carrier, offering prayers or a gentle hand.

A Hindu redeeming vows carries a *kavadi* ("kah-vah-dee"). This is a fancifully decorated structure that is balanced on skewers inserted into the bearer's back and arms or attached to the flesh by steel hooks and chains. To increase the penance, additional skewers may be stuck through the penitent's cheeks or tongue.

The amazing part of a *kavadi* procession is not how seemingly easily the entranced penitents carry their burdens, but the fact that half an hour after the event, when the skewers have been removed, the penitents appear to have sustained neither wounds nor swellings on their bodies!

The most famous procession is held at Kuala Lumpur's Batu Caves, where 800,000 spectators gather to watch penitents climb the 272 steps up to a shrine housed in a limestone cave.

Dressed in traditional costumes of black and gold, Kadazans dance and chant at the Magavan rites performed during the Harvest Festival. They are led by a priestess, or *bobohizan* ("boh-boh-hee-zahn"). In Kadazan society, it is the women who play significant roles in traditional rituals.

KADAZAN HARVEST FESTIVAL

This harvest festival is celebrated in the East Malaysian state of Sabah. While it has been named after Sabah's major indigenous tribe, the Kadazan, all Sabah natives keep the solemnity and everyone else joins in the festivities.

This holiday is based on the Kadazan's worship of ancient gods, including the rice spirit Bambaazon, who is revered in rice plants, rice grains, and cooked rice. Without rice there is no life. Kadazan children are taught from an early age never to spill or waste any of the precious grain and to pay special respects to the gods whenever the village reaps a good rice harvest.

The harvest festival is a time when many Sabah natives take their traditional clothes out of the closet and put them on for a few days. The event is celebrated with public gatherings and family parties and an open house to all visitors. *Air tapai* ("ah-yay tah-pie"), a homemade rice wine, is freely given to all.

GAWAI DAYAK

The Gawai Dayak has only been celebrated as a public holiday since 1964. Previously Sarawak's indigenous tribes held their own harvest festivals at their own times, but with the establishment of the Gawai, the celebrations have been put on an official footing.

Gawai is held in towns as well as in longhouses, with traditional costume parades and competitions. For some people this is the only time in the year they wear their beautiful but somewhat cumbersome traditional outfits. The Gawai showcases the Iban women's silver jewelry and the Orang Ulus' priceless antique beads.

Gawai Dayak is celebrated with an open house, official parties and receptions, and streams of *tuak* ("too-ahk"), a homemade rice wine. In longhouses, offerings of food are made to the gods of rice and prosperity and blessed by waving a chicken over the display.

Gawai is celebrated by the Jagoi Dayak in western Sarawak. The elders, seated and partaking of a meal "on behalf of the ancestral spirits," are leaders of the tribal cult. The women guard the *padi* seed in covered baskets. This grain will be used to plant the fields a few months after Gawai.

113

Hari Raya Puasa is an opportunity for relatives and friends to meet and catch up with one another over delightful cookies and cakes.

MUSLIM FESTIVALS

HARI RAYA PUASA This marks the end of the fasting month of Ramadan, when for 30 days Muslims take no food or drink from dawn to dusk.

Before Hari Raya Puasa, houses are cleaned and given a new coat of paint. New curtains are made, new clothes sewn, and huge quantities of special foods are prepared.

On Hari Raya morning, the men and boys in the family go to the mosque for prayers, after which the family visits the graves of their departed loved ones. The rest of the day is spent visiting the homes of friends and relatives where a colorful array of food is served.

HARI RAYA HAJI This festival commemorates Ibrahim's (Abraham's) willingness to sacrifice his son Ismail (Ishmael) at Allah's (God's) bidding. It is celebrated in particular by Muslims who have made the *haj* ("hahj"), the required pilgrimage to Mecca. The men attend the Hari Raya Haji prayers at the mosque, after which some of the worshipers perform animal sacrifices. For Muslims making the *haj*, prayers offered on this day mark the end of the pilgrimage.

MA'AL HIJRAH (AWAL MUHARRAM) Ma'al Hijrah is the first day on the Islamic calendar, that is, it marks the start of the new year for Muslims. More importantly, it is the anniversary of the Prophet Mohammed's flight from Mecca to Medina. Ma'al Hijrah commemorates the beginning of Islam as a separate religion.

According to this reckoning, 2000 was the year 1421H until the date of Ma'al Hijrah sometime in April. The year 1422H started on March 26, 2001, which was also the first day of the month of Muharram.

PROPHET MOHAMMED'S BIRTHDAY The birthday of the founder of Islam, Prophet Mohammed, is commemorated by Muslims. It falls on the 12th day of the month of Rabiulawal, which was June 4 in 2001. As a public holiday, Prophet Mohammed's birthday is celebrated with special prayers, processions, and religious rallies.

OTHER FESTIVALS

Other major festivals celebrated in Malaysia include Vesak Day, a celebration of Buddha's birth, death, and enlightenment, when Buddhists make visits to the temples to offer prayers; Chinese All Souls' Day, a day set aside by the Chinese to visit and clean the ancestral graves and offer food to the spirits of their ancestors; Deepavali, an important Hindu festival celebrated by Hindu Indians; and Christmas, though it is not celebrated in as big a way as in the United States—in Malaysia, it is more a time of super sales at department stores.

Hari Raya Haji is also known as Hari Raya Korban, the festival of sacrifice, in commemoration of the sacrifice Ibrahim offered to Allah in place of his son, Ismail. On Hari Raya Haji, Muslim men slaughter animals, usually sheep, at the mosque and distribute the meat to the poor.

FOOD

"HAVE YOU EATEN YOUR RICE?" is a common greeting in Malaysia. Most Malaysians eat rice at least once a day. Other foods are cooked to "give flavor to the rice." Malaysians serve food and dine in many ways. They may use a pair of chopsticks and eat out of a bowl, spread their food out on a banana leaf and eat with their fingers, or eat with a fork and a spoon from a plate.

Fresh food is available all year round. Careful homemakers buy fresh greens and small amounts of fresh meat or fish from the wet market on a daily basis. Grocery shopping has become a little more popular, but the wet market, with its fresh produce and negotiable prices, is still by far the best place to shop for everyday food items.

Fish is a universal favorite in Malaysia. Everyone, young and old, may fish with lines or baskets or set fish traps. Many coastal farmers moonlight as part-time fishermen. It is no wonder that fish is so popular. People of all religions can eat fish, and connoisseurs claim that fish does not seem to have the "smell" that meat has. Meat is almost always cooked in soups or the ubiquitous curry and cut into bite-sized pieces before serving. The Western style of bringing a whole roast chicken to the table for the master of the house to carve strikes Malaysians as strange. As for steaks … how would you tackle them with chopsticks or your fingers?

Above: **A stall in the market selling fresh fish.**

Opposite: **Typical Straits Chinese dishes—a lip-smacking combination of Chinese food spiced Malay-style.**

Above: **Nowadays the Chinese use the traditional charcoal stove only for brewing herbal soups and simmering smooth *congee* ("conjee"), or porridge.**

Below: **A longhouse hearth. Fish is being cooked in the bamboo tubes (bottom right).**

WHAT'S COOKING?

In towns, bottled gas or electricity is used for cooking. In Miri, Sarawak, gas is piped throughout the town and sold to consumers at a cheap rate. Microwave ovens, electric rice cookers, and toasters—all the labor-saving kitchen devices of modern times—have made their appearance in Malaysian kitchens.

In the countryside, many homemakers have gas stoves too, although some still use kerosene burners. The traditional village hearth is a clay slab placed on the kitchen floor or on a ledge. Here a fire is kindled in the morning and the cooking pots placed over it on iron tripods or stones. Fish or whatever is to be cooked is laid across green branches to grill or suspended at a height to smoke.

The old-fashioned Chinese housewife uses a charcoal stove, a round pot with a small grate in which a charcoal fire is fanned to life. Not many households today rely entirely on this fuel. But should a power outage occur, the homemaker may be glad to have a charcoal pot substitute sitting in the corner of the kitchen.

Strict Hindus belonging to the high castes have complicated and demanding dietary laws, one of which demands that all their food be cooked in pure brass pots. The modern alternative is stainless steel. Some families keep one set of utensils for the orthodox members and a separate one for the more liberal.

Young Malaysian women of all ethnicities are advised not to sing in the kitchen. It will not affect the food, but the musical cook will be destined to marry an old man!

TABLE MANNERS

Table manners are not strictly restricted to the table. Many Malaysians eat on clean mats spread on the floor, and they are quite as conscious of decorum as anybody else.

An essential rule, especially among Muslims, is that only the right hand may be used for eating. It is washed in fresh water before the meal. The left hand is considered unclean because it is used to clean oneself after a visit to the restroom. The right hand is used to scoop up rice, pick tidbits from the various cooked dishes, or roll up a morsel of *sambal belacan* ("sahm-bahl beh-lah-chahn")—a condiment of prawn paste, ground chili peppers, and lime juice—in a blanched leaf. The little finger is not used for holding food; the others only up to the second knuckle. Soup is served in individual bowls and eaten with a spoon.

After the meal, a dish of water is passed around; small children may have to wash their whole hand but anybody with good manners need only rinse the thumb and three fingers.

Casual visitors are asked to partake of any meal the family may be having. If they are formally invited guests, they may be served separately from the family.

In conservative households, the women and children eat by themselves after the men have had their fill. It is a matter of some importance for a boy to be promoted to eat with his father. This may be after he has passed important school examinations or some other such rite of passage.

The "eating order" may even be extended—men eat first, women and little children who need help with eating next. School-age children and servants eat last.

Many Malaysians eat with their fingers, while sitting on clean mats on the floor.

Rice has to be treated respectfully. The grains are carried from the storage jar in a little basket. Scooping them straight into the cooking pot is an insult. Cooked rice can be served on individual plates or in a big bowl, but the rice pot must not be brought to the table.

FOOD TABOOS

The most obvious food taboo in an officially Muslim nation is the prohibition on pork. Pork-free food is certified *halal* ("hah-lahl") to indicate to Muslim customers that it is not forbidden.

Hindus and Sikhs do not eat beef, although they use milk products in their diets. Some Hindus also avoid eggs; others consume only food that does not involve killing. Buddhists avoid dairy products, such as egg, butter, and cheese. They get protein from soy beans and other vegetable products such as lentils.

Such restrictions can be a headache when cooking for a special function such as a party. It is normal to ask guests if they eat pork or beef to sort out what may be served to each guest.

An unexpected visitor at mealtime must be offered food. He will probably decline, but he must touch a little rice offered to him on a spoon. Refusing rice carries a penalty: the churl will be bitten by a snake or scorpion on his way home!

Home-cooked fare is eaten without comment. Sniffing food is regarded as very rude by most Malaysians. Refusing food by touching the dish with the right hand is acceptable.

The Murut drink *air tapai* through reed straws from earthenware jars used to age the brew.

DRINKING

Muslims do not drink alcohol. However beer can be purchased in most urbanized areas of Malaysia and is drunk by the Chinese and Indians. In certain rural areas of Malaysia, such as the eastern coast of the peninsula, it is quite common to find signs stating "Muslims will not be served alcohol" in coffeeshops and restaurants.

Some Malaysians like to brew their own alcohol. A kind of wine called toddy can be made from sugarcane juice and the sap of several palms, such as the coconut and the *nipah* ("nee-pah"). The bud stems of the palm are slightly cut and the juice oozing out is collected in small vessels, then emptied into a jar and fermented with or without the addition of yeast. Good toddy is refreshing and slightly lighter than beer.

Borneo natives make a sort of beer out of cooked glutinous rice and homemade yeast. It tastes not unlike Japanese *sake* ("sah-kay"), although the quality is seldom standard. The drink is called *tuak* or *air tapai*.

Rice beer and toddy can be distilled into high-grade alcohol called *arrak* ("ah-rahk"). Unskilled processing or the addition of other substances can make this homemade beverage dangerous. Cases of death and serious illness from drinking *arrak* have occasionally been reported.

Convivial Malaysians of Chinese origin try to speed up their guests' consumption of liquor or soft drinks with shouts of *yam seng* (bottoms up)!

Malaysians like company when drinking. Some communities have "drinking songs." Among these, the chants of Sarawak's Kayans holds a special place. They originated when a high-ranking chief of old refused to drink unless the woman offering him the glass sang a song and everyone else present repeated the chorus!

An *ulam* meal. Clockwise from top left: cabbage, *kacang botol*, *buah jering*, pounded dried prawns, chilies, *ikan parang* (wolf herring), *chin char loke*, *sambal belacan*, *buah petai*, and cucumber.

AN ULAM SPREAD

Visitors to Malaysia might occasionally see adults or children picking an oily-looking creeper leaf from a hedge or an inconspicuous fern shoot from the undergrowth by the side of the road. "To *ulam* ("ooh-lahm") with our lunch!" they explain to a curious passerby.

Ulam is a popular dish among Malaysians, regardless of ethnicity. An *ulam* spread consists largely of prawn, fish, and a variety of vegetables, including leaves, creepers, beans, cucumber, and cabbage. Every Malaysian child knows how to pick out the edible shoots from the inedible ones. To top it all off, a spicy sauce called *sambal* adds spike to the spread. *Nasi ulam* is made by frying rice with shredded vegetables, sliced chillies, fish flakes, and small prawns.

Sometimes *ulam* vegetables are blanched in boiling water for a minute or so. In a dysentery-prone area where raw food often carries germs, this is a wise precaution.

The absence of meat makes *ulam* especially appropriate for the Muslim menu, as Muslims are not allowed to eat pork, or meat that has not been slaughtered in the name of Allah.

BEGEDIL

This is an easy-to-make local version of the potato cutlet.

1 large potato
2 tablespoons oil
$\frac{1}{2}$ teaspoon nutmeg
1 egg, beaten

$\frac{1}{2}$ medium-sized onion
$\frac{1}{2}$ stalk celery
pinch of salt

1. Boil and mash potato.
2. Finely slice onion and fry in one tablespoon of oil until brown and fragrant.
3. Chop celery coarsely.
4. Mix well-mashed potato, onion, celery, nutmeg, and salt. Divide dough-like mixture into six portions. Form each portion into a small ball, then flatten to $\frac{1}{2}$-inch thickness.
5. Heat remainder of oil in skillet. Dip each cutlet into beaten egg before putting into pan. Fry cutlets until golden brown, remove, and drain on paper towels.
6. Serve hot with lettuce and tomatoes.

WEDDING FEASTS

In most cultures, weddings are occasions to have a feast. However solemn the ceremony may be, once the priests and elders have performed the rites, everyone adjourns to a sumptuous feast. In rural areas, the whole village participates in a wedding, but urban couples send their wedding invitations only to as many family members and friends as the budget will allow. Some Malaysian parents, however, are willing to incur heavy debts just to give their son or daughter a grand wedding party.

An important part of Malay wedding plans concerns money matters: who will pay for what and how much can be spent? In rural areas, the groom's contribution is brought to the bride's house in a merry procession of unmarried girls carrying decorated foodstuffs and banknotes pleated into flowers. As a token of their mutual caring and sharing, the bride and groom are made to "feed" each other after the wedding ceremony.

Chinese couples announce their engagement by distributing a special kind of sweet among their families and friends. It is made of finely ground peanuts and spun sugar, often packed together with slabs of peanut toffee. Love is sweet! The wedding dinner itself may consist of 10 or 12 courses, each one finer (and more expensive) than the one before.

The feast for a Sikh wedding is prepared by the community's elders in the temple. The main work of catering is the responsibility of a team of stalwart men, who are experts in the production of unleavened bread and huge tubs of curry.

A rural Malay wedding procession bearing decorated foodstuffs and other gifts to the house of the bride.

PICNIC FOOD

In some cultures, a picnic means sandwiches and an easy day for the cook; Malaysians take picnics much more seriously.

Food always means rice, regardless of where you are in Malaysia. Whether the picnickers are a busload of students or Boy Scouts on a field trip or a sports or fishing group having a gathering, they are sure to make provisions for cooking and eating rice. On arriving at the picnic spot, the party builds a little fire. The more responsible members of the group then begin boiling the rice and pounding the spices for the *sambal*. Then the food is served on large leaves plucked from a tree and wiped cleaned. Eating is done with the fingers.

Nasi lemak—coconut rice with egg, cucumber, fish, and spicy condiments—is favorite picnic fare. It is delicious hot or cold.

Some Malaysian picnickers bring cold cooked rice packed with a spicy condiment in a large banana leaf. Called *nasi lemak* ("nah-si leh-mah"), this used to be the classic fare to take on school picnics, and the preparation of so many picnic packs at a go required a lot of patience and had to begin long before dawn.

A Malaysian seaside picnic may take the whole weekend. The members of the group bring along fishing tackle, hooks and lines, nets, and crab traps. Their freshly caught seafood and fish are flipped from the line or net on to a rough little grill constructed out of green sticks to be roasted to perfection. An upcountry picnic party does not rely on its guns for provisions. To supplement or substitute for a fresh catch, canned foods are carried along, in particular *ikan sardin* ("ee-kahn sahr-din")—canned mackerel or tuna.

Rice dumplings wrapped in bamboo leaves are offered to the gods and eaten during the Dragon Boat Festival in remembrance of Chinese poet and patriot Qu Yuan.

Qu Yuan, who lived in the third century B.C., committed suicide by jumping into the Milu River, because he could not bear to see his state suffer defeat by enemies. The peasantry, on hearing the news, went out on the river in boats to look for his body. They could not find it and began beating drums and throwing rice dumplings into the river to keep the fish away from the body. Thus began a tradition that is kept to this day—making rice dumplings and holding dragon boat races on the fifth day of the fifth lunar month.

Stories abound about the origin of Deepavali, the festival of lights. But whichever story the Hindu subscribes to, *mithai* ("mee-thai"), or sweets, are a very important part of the celebration. Sweets, revered by the Hindus as food for the gods, are offered to deities and exchanged as a symbol of happiness and an act of goodwill. On this day too, lamps are lit at the entrance of the home, and *kollam* ("koh-lahm")—patterns traced out in rice—are created at the main door and entrance to the worship room.

FOOD CAN BE GOOD FOR THE SOUL

Special sweets tell the world that a Chinese couple is engaged. A triangular rice dumpling is given to friends on the day of the Dragon Boat Festival. Romantic stories are told about the plump, rich moon cakes exchanged during the Moon Cake Festival.

The Bidayuh of Sarawak have a new year's ceremony during which a member from each household sets out with a basket full of rice cakes and presents each family in the village with one piece. While the messenger is out, an emissary from every family in the village similarly visits his or her house, returning the same present many times over.

At the Gawai, a harvest festival celebrated by Borneo natives, visitors are not only royally feasted but are also pressed to take basketfuls of special cakes home with them. Let nobody say the hosts are stingy!

A Malay rice cake, the *ketupat* ("keh-too-paht"), is steamed in a square case of coconut leaf. For festive occasions, the cases can be fashioned into fish or bird shapes, designs limited only by the skill of the manufacturer. During holiday seasons, there are *ketupat*-making contests in some villages, emphasizing either speed or beauty.

Indian foods for festival consumption are beautifully colored and sometimes decorated with paper-thin pieces of gold or silver. On the occasion of Deepavali, the festival of lights, the dividing line between food and art is blurred: one of the most beautiful decorations consists of large, intricate designs drawn on the floor with colored rice.

Ketupat, a rice cake cooked in coconut leaf. Before serving, the rice cake is cut in half and each half is then further cut into smaller pieces. It is then served on a plate with the coconut leaf casing.

EATING OUT IN MALAYSIA

With a climate that favors outdoor activity and a gregarious nature, Malaysians enjoy eating out all year round at a range of food centers and restaurants with Malay, Chinese, Indian, and international fare.

The bigger towns have hawker centers where dozens of individual cooks set up little kitchens to prepare rice, noodles, fish and meat dishes, vegetarian selections, sweet and spicy dishes—any dish imaginable—while you wait at one of the tables. Traveling hawkers offer most urban neighborhoods steamed dumplings, a variety of noodle dishes cooked on portable stoves, grilled meat, ice cream, and cold drinks.

Under the shade of leafy trees, food vendors dish out local favorites from their kitchens-on-wheels.

A small town, a ferry point, or a river jetty is sure to have at least a couple of noodle stalls and a drink vendor, maybe a "coconut man" who lops the top off the green globe and extracts the fruit's sweet water for sale.

Malaysians even like going out for breakfast. In the cool of the morning, they congregate around small tables under trees or big umbrella shades outside coffee shops. Rice gruel spooned boiling hot over a raw egg is a favorite. Salted and fried tidbits are eaten with this as a relish to add flavor. Noodles of different shapes and colors—long, flat, fat, stringy, white, yellow—are prepared to customers' tastes and served with soup or dry, bland or fiercely spiced. Breakfast "bread" is available in the form of Indian pancakes eaten with meat or lentil curry sauces. Malaysians with conservative tastes enjoy *nasi lemak* for breakfast too.

Halal restaurants serving international cuisines—Italian, Japanese, Mexican, Vietnamese, Mediterranean, North Indian, Thai—may be the choice for less casual outings.

FAST FOOD

Fast food is catching on quickly in Malaysia. In many towns, there is now a hamburger joint, although the product is called a beefburger to reassure Muslim customers that there is no pork in it. Chicken restaurants of the Colonel Sanders type are common sights in urban shopping malls. Youngsters relish the freedom of a place not frequented by older folk. Office workers who can live without rice "grab a bite" instead of going home for lunch.

McDonald's and Kentucky Fried Chicken outlets are decorated and managed like their prototypes in the United States, except that the language is, of course, Malay. Western fast food has become a popular option among Malaysians, besides also being a comfortable retreat for Western tourists looking for the familiar meal of a burger, french fries, and Coca-Cola.

Ronald welcomes visitors at the entrance of a McDonald's outlet in Malaysia.

Fast food does not have to be foreign though. Malaysians can get local food fast at canteen-style restaurants. There is no need to place an order and then wait for it to be cooked. Food here is cooked and ready. Each customer simply asks for a plate of rice and then chooses two to four side dishes from heated display trays. There is usually a wide variety of curries, vegetables, and fried foods like fish, eggs, and peanuts to choose from.

Many rural secondary schools in Malaysia have boarding facilities. Food here is cooked in large quantities and often eaten in shifts, depending on the size of the mess hall. Each student gets a mound of rice with a few simple side dishes for flavor and nutrition.

NASI LEMAK

This is coconut rice served with spicy sidedishes. See picture on page 125.

10.6 oz (300 g) long grain rice
2 shallots
2 slices peeled ginger

1/8 tsp fenugreek (fennel) seeds
1 teaspoon salt
1.7 cups (400 ml) coconut milk

Rinse rice until clean. Place drained rice into a rice cooker together with shallots, ginger, fenugreek seeds, and salt. Pour in coconut milk to a depth of 0.8 inch (2 cm) over rice. Cook mixture until dry. Use a wooden spoon to loosen grains. Sprinkle remaining coconut milk over rice. Stir with a pair of chopsticks to distribute milk evenly. Leave to stand for 10 to 15 minutes. Keep warm.

Preparing the anchovy sidedish

3.5 oz (100 g) soaked anchovies
3 tablespoons oil

1 sliced Bombay onion
2 tablespoons chili paste

Pounded ingredients
5 shallots
2 cloves garlic
1 thinly sliced stalk lemon grass
1/2 tsp chili granules

Seasoning
1/2 teaspoon anchovy granules
1 teaspoon sugar or to taste
2 tablespoons lime juice
2 tablespoons water

Heat oil in a frying pan. Saute pounded ingredients, chili paste, and chili granules until fragrant. Add anchovies and onions. Stir-fry well. Mix in lime juice, water, and seasoning ingredients. Mix well. Serve with rice.

Preparing the prawn sidedish

10.6 oz (300 g) shelled medium-sized prawns
3-4 tablespoons oil

Ground ingredients
5 dried chilies, soaked
2 fresh red chilies, seeded

Seasoning
1/2 tablespoon sugar or to taste
1/2 teaspoon salt or to taste
1/4 teaspoon chicken bouillon granules

4 shallots
2 cloves garlic
1/4 teaspoon chili granules
Juice of 2 large limes

Heat oil in a frying pan. Saute ground ingredients until aromatic. Add prawns and cook for three to four minutes. Stir in lime juice and seasonings. Stir-fry well. Serve with rice.

SATAY CITARASA

10.6 oz (300 g) boneless beef
10.6 oz (300 g) chicken fillet
2 tablespoons oil

14 oz (400 g) squid
Bamboo skewers, soaked overnight

Ground spices
10 shallots
0.8 inches (2 cm) piece fresh turmeric
1.6 inches (4 cm) galangale
1.2 inches (3 cm) fresh ginger
1/2 teaspoon ground fennel seed
1/2 teaspoon coriander powder
1 tablespoon chili paste

Seasoning
2 tablespoons brown sugar
1 teaspoon salt or to taste
1 teaspoon soy sauce
3 tablespoons honey
2 tablespoons coconut milk

Cut the beef, squid (remove the ink bags), and chicken fillet into strips 0.8 inch (2 cm) long. Marinate the meat and squid with the ground spices and seasonings (reserve some for the glaze). Refrigerate, preferably overnight, then add two tablespoons of oil to the marinated ingredients. Thread the meat and squid onto the skewers. Grill or barbecue the meat until dark brown.

Preparing the sauce

1 tablespoon fresh chili paste
2 tablespoons dried chili paste
8 minced shallots
5 cloves garlic, ground
1 teaspoon chili granules
1/2 cup coconut milk

1/2 cup lime juice
3 tablespoons sugar
1 teaspoon salt or to taste
1/2 cup roasted peanuts, coarsely ground
1 stalk lemon grass, smashed
4 tablespoons oil

Heat the oil in a wok and fry the ingredients and lemon grass until aromatic. Add the coconut milk and lime juice. Bring to a gentle boil and simmer until the oil rises to the top. Stir in the ground peanuts, sugar, and salt. Serve with the grilled or barbequed meat.

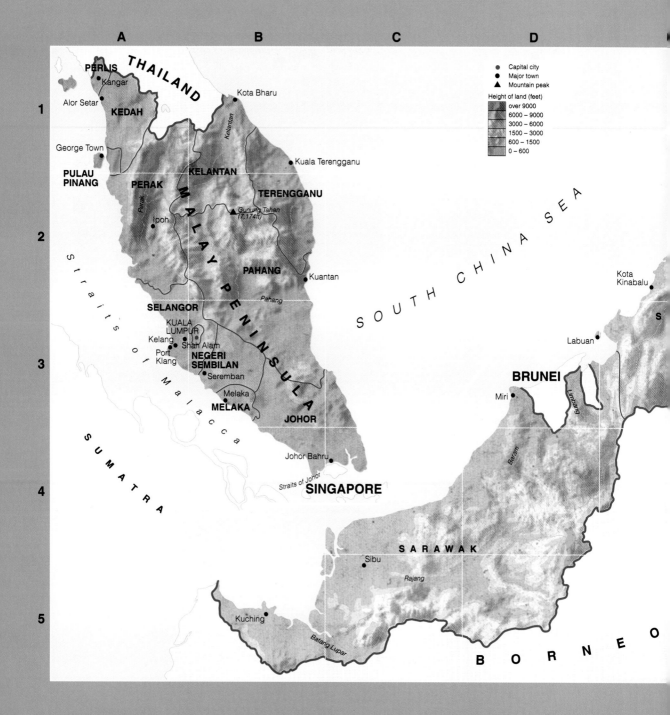

MAP OF MALAYSIA

F

N

Sulu Sea

Sandakan

Sulawesi Sea

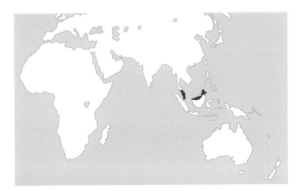

ECONOMIC MALAYSI

PERLIS
• Kangar
Alor Setar •
KEDAH
• Kota Bharu

George Town •
PENANG
PERAK
KELANTAN
• Ipoh
• Cameron
Highlands
TERENGGANU
• Kuala
Terengganu

PAHANG
• Kuantan

SELANGOR
KUALA
LUMPUR
Kelang •
Shah
Alam •
NEGERI
SEMBILAN
• Tasek
Dampar
• Seremban
Port •
Dickson •
Melaka •
MELAKA
JOHOR

• Johor Bahru

Labuan •

Miri •

Bintulu •

SARAWAK

Sibu •

Kuching •

Natural Resources

Rubber
Fish
Oil
Tea
Timber
Fruit & Vegetables

Services

Port
Airport

ABOUT THE ECONOMY

GROSS DOMESTIC PRODUCT
US$227 billion (2000)

GDP SECTORS
Services 43%, industry 40%, and agriculture 17%

MINERAL RESOURCES
Tin, petroleum, copper, iron, natural gas, and bauxite

AGRICULTURAL PRODUCTS
Rubber, palm oil, rice, subsistence crops, timber, coconut, and pepper

WORKFORCE
9.3 million

EMPLOYMENT PROFILE
Industry 36%, services 42%, agriculture 16%, and others 6%

UNEMPLOYMENT RATE
3 percent

CURRENCY
US$1 = RM3.80 (Jan 2000)
1 ringgit (RM) = 100 cents

INFLATION RATE
2.8 percent (2000)

PORTS & HARBORS
Bintulu, Kota Kinabalu, Kuantan, Kuching, Labuan, Melaka, Penang, Port Dickson, Sibu, Sandakan, and Tawau

AIRPORTS
115 (32 with paved runways)

MAJOR IMPORTS
Machinery, equipment, chemicals, and food

MAJOR EXPORTS
Electronic equipment, petroleum, petroleum products, palm oil, wood, wood products, rubber, and textiles

TRADING PARTNERS
Singapore, Japan, Hong Kong, Thailand, Taiwan, China, South Korea, the Netherlands, and the United States.

HIGHWAYS
58,720 miles (94,500 km)

RAILWAYS
1,117 miles (1,798 km)

WATERWAYS
4,534 miles (7,296 km)

CULTURAL MALAYSIA

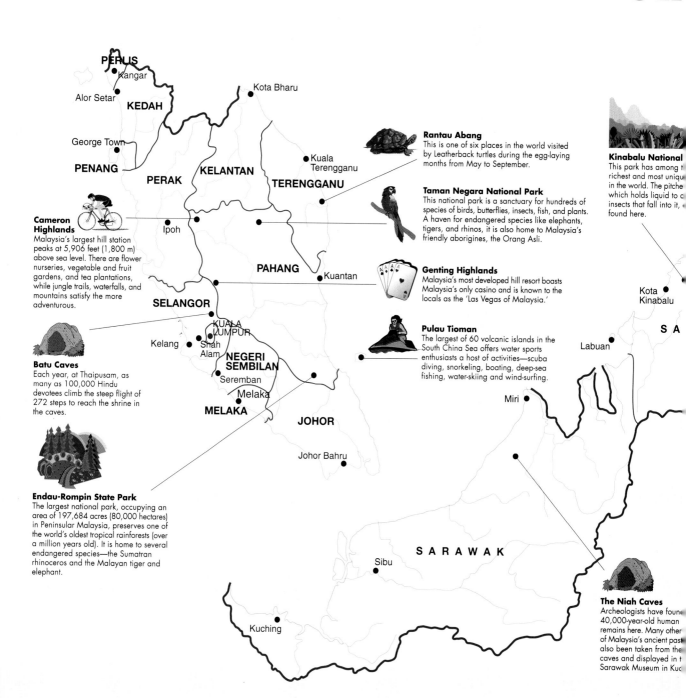

PERLIS
Kangar
Alor Setar
KEDAH
George Town
PENANG
PERAK
Kota Bharu
KELANTAN
Kuala Terengganu
TERENGGANU
Ipoh
PAHANG
Kuantan
SELANGOR
KUALA LUMPUR
Kelang
Shah Alam
NEGERI SEMBILAN
Seremban
Melaka
MELAKA
JOHOR
Johor Bahru
Kuching
Sibu
SARAWAK
Miri
Labuan
Kota Kinabalu
S A

Rantau Abang
This is one of six places in the world visited by Leatherback turtles during the egg-laying months from May to September.

Taman Negara National Park
This national park is a sanctuary for hundreds of species of birds, butterflies, insects, fish, and plants. A haven for endangered species like elephants, tigers, and rhinos, it is also home to Malaysia's friendly aborigines, the Orang Asli.

Kinabalu National
This park has among the richest and most unique in the world. The pitche which holds liquid to c insects that fall into it, found here.

Cameron Highlands
Malaysia's largest hill station peaks at 5,906 feet (1,800 m) above sea level. There are flower nurseries, vegetable and fruit gardens, and tea plantations, while jungle trails, waterfalls, and mountains satisfy the more adventurous.

Genting Highlands
Malaysia's most developed hill resort boasts Malaysia's only casino and is known to the locals as the 'Las Vegas of Malaysia.'

Pulau Tioman
The largest of 60 volcanic islands in the South China Sea offers water sports enthusiasts a host of activities—scuba diving, snorkeling, boating, deep-sea fishing, water-skiing and wind-surfing.

Batu Caves
Each year, at Thaipusam, as many as 100,000 Hindu devotees climb the steep flight of 272 steps to reach the shrine in the caves.

Endau-Rompin State Park
The largest national park, occupying an area of 197,684 acres (80,000 hectares) in Peninsular Malaysia, preserves one of the world's oldest tropical rainforests (over a million years old). It is home to several endangered species—the Sumatran rhinoceros and the Malayan tiger and elephant.

The Niah Caves
Archeologists have foun 40,000-year-old human remains here. Many other of Malaysia's ancient pas also been taken from the caves and displayed in t Sarawak Museum in Kuc

ABOUT THE CULTURE

Sepilok Orangutan Sanctuary
Sepilok is one of four orangutan sanctuaries in the world. Covering 4,000 hectares (9,884 acres), the center looks after captive orangutans to help them adjust gradually to living in the wild.

Sandakan

Tawau

OFFICIAL NAME
Malaysia

CAPITAL
Kuala Lumpur

FLAG
Fourteen horizontal red and white stripes with a blue rectangle in the upper hoist-edge corner bearing a yellow crescent and star, traditional symbols of Islam.

NATIONAL ANTHEM
Negara Ku ("My Country")

POPULATION
21,793,293 (2000 est.)

LIFE EXPECTANCY
70.67 years

ETHNIC GROUPS
Malays and other indigenous 58%, Chinese 26%, Indians 7%, Others 9%.

RELIGIONS
Islam (national), Buddhism, Hinduism, Taoism, Christianity, Sikhism. Shamanism is also practiced in East Malaysia.

LITERACY RATE
93 percent (1998)

LANGUAGES & DIALECTS
Bahasa Malaysia, English, Cantonese, Mandarin, Hokkien, Hakka, Tamil, Telugu, Malayalam, Punjabi. Indigenous languages, such as Iban and Kadazan, are also spoken in East Malaysia.

HOLIDAYS & FESTIVALS
Fixed dates: New Year's Day (Jan 1), Labor Day (May 1), National Day (Aug 31), Christmas (Dec 25). Variable dates: Chinese New Year, Hari Raya Puasa, Hari Raya Haji, Good Friday, Easter, Vesak Day, Thaipusam, Deepavali.

TIME
Greenwich Mean Time plus 8 hours (GMT+0800)

SYSTEM OF GOVERNMENT
Constitutional monarchy headed by a paramount ruler and a parliament consisting of a nonelected upper house and an elected lower house. Each state, except Melaka, Penang, Sabah, and Sarawak, has a hereditary ruler.

LEADERS IN POLITICS
Tunku Abdul Rahman (1903–1990)—first prime minister of Malaysia
Prime Minister Dr. Mahathir bin Mohamad

TIME LINE

IN MALAYSIA	IN THE WORLD
	753 B.C. Rome founded
200 B.C. Beginning of trade with India and China	
	116–17 B.C. Roman Empire reaches its greatest extent, under Emperor Trajan (98–17 B.C.).
100 B.C. – A.D. 200 Emergence of trading kingdoms in the Isthmus of Kra	
500 – 1000 Development of trade on Bujang Valley and in northern Perak.	**A.D. 600** Height of Mayan civilization
1400 Palembang prince Parameswara founds Melaka.	**1000** Chinese perfect gunpowder and begin to use it in warfare.
1511 A Portuguese fleet captures Melaka.	
	1530 Beginning of trans-Atlantic slave trade organized by Portuguese in Africa
	1558 – 1603 Reign of Elizabeth I of England
	1620 Pilgrim Fathers sail the Mayflower to America
1641 The Dutch take over Melaka.	
	1776 U. S. Declaration of Independence
1786 The British East India Company acquires Penang.	**1789 – 1799** The French Revolution
1819 Sir Stamford Raffles founds Singapore.	
1824 Anglo-Dutch treaty transfers control of Melaka to Britain.	
1826 Penang, Melaka, and Singapore form the Straits Settlements.	**1861** U. S. Civil War begins.
1896 Perak, Selangor, Negeri Sembilan, and Pahang form the Federated Malay States.	**1869** The Suez Canal is opened.

IN MALAYSIA	IN THE WORLD

1909
Kedah, Trengganu, Kelantan, and Perlis form the Unfederated Malay States.

1914
World War I begins.

1939
World War II begins.

1941–1945
The Japanese occupy Malaysia.

1945
The United States drops atomic bombs on Hiroshima and Nagasaki.

1946
Dato Onn bin Ja'afar founds the United Malays National Organization (UMNO).

1948
The Federation of Malaya is formed, consisting of the Malay States and the Straits Settlements. The Communist Party of Malaya begins a guerilla insurgency to defeat the colonial government, sparking off a 12-year state of emergency.

1949
North Atlantic Treaty Organization (NATO) formed

1955
The Alliance Party wins 51 of 52 seats in the first general elections and sets up the first government.

1957
Malaya gains independence. Tunku Abdul Rahman becomes the first prime minister.

1957
Russians launch Sputnik.

1963
Sarawak, Sabah, and Singapore join Malaya to form the Federation of Malaysia.

1965
Singapore leaves the Federation.

1966 – 1969
Chinese Cultural Revolution

1967
Malaysia and Singapore establish the Association of Southeast Asian Nations (ASEAN).

1970
Tun Abdul Razak becomes prime minister. The New Economic Policy era begins.

1981
Mahathir bin Mohamad becomes prime minister.

1986
Nuclear power disaster at Chernobyl in Ukraine

1991
The New Development Policy is implemented.

1991
Break-up of Soviet Union

1997
Malaysia is hit by the Asian economic crisis.

1997
Hong Kong is returned to China.

1999
Mahathir is elected prime minister for the fifth time.

2001
World population surpasses 6 billion.

GLOSSARY

agong ("ah-gong")
A king.

amah ("ah-mah")
A paid housemaid.

ang pow ("ahng-pow")
A small red paper envelope containing money given as a gift at birthdays, weddings, and the Lunar New Year.

Apa khabar? ("ah-pah khah-bahr?")
How are you?

Aurea Chersonesus
Malaya's old name, meaning "peninsula of gold."

baju ("bah-joo")
Clothing.

batik ("bah-tick")
A fabric printed with colorful dyes.

bumiputera ("boo-MI-put-teh-RAH")
Native Malays; literally "princes of the soil."

haj
Muslim pilgrimage to Mecca.

halal
Can be eaten by Muslims; *halal* food has no pork and is specially prepared.

ikat ("ee-kaht")
A uniquely patterned fabric woven by the Iban people of Sarawak.

joss sticks
Incense sticks lighted by Buddhists when they pray.

kampung ("kahm-pohng")
A village.

kota ("koh-tah")
A town or city.

Orang Asli
Tribes living in the interior rural parts of Malaysia.

orangutan
An intelligent red ape; literally "forest people."

pantun ("pahn-toon")
Malay verse.

puasa ("poo-ah-sah")
To fast; Muslims eat nothing between breakfast and dinner during the month of Ramadan.

Qu'ran ("kooh-rahn")
Islam's holy book.

songkok ("sohng-koh")
A (usually) black cap worn by Muslim men to the mosque.

FURTHER INFORMATION

BOOKS

Insight Guide: Malaysia. Singapore: APA Publications, 2000.

Major, John S. *The Land and People of Malaysia and Brunei*. New York: HarperCollins , 1991.

Malaysia in Pictures. Minneapolis: Lerner Publications, 1989.

Munan, Heidi. *Culture Shock! Malaysia*. Oregon: Graphic Arts Center Publishing Company, 1991.

Oon, Helen. *Globetrotter Travel Guides: Malaysia*. London: New Holland Publishers, 2000.

Payne, Junaidi and Gerald Cubitt (photographer). *Wild Malaysia: The Wildlife and Scenery of Peninsular Malaysia, Sarawak and Sabah*. Massachusetts: MIT Press, 1990.

Toynbee, Manson and Mary W. Toynbee. *Jungle Schools: Letters from Sarawak 1958-1965*. Salt Spring Island: M. Hepburn & Associates, 1997.

Watson Andaya, Barbara and Leonard Y. Andaya. *A History of Malaysia*. Hawai'i: University of Hawai'i Press, 2001.

WEBSITES

Central Intelligence Agency World Factbook (select Malaysia from the country list).
www.odci.gov/cia/publications/factbook/index.html

Lonely Planet World Guide: Destination Malaysia.
www.lonelyplanet.com/destinations/south_east_asia/malaysia/

Malaysia Homepage. www.interknowledge.com/malaysia

Malaysian National Library. www.pnm.my

Ministry of International Trade and Industry (MITI). www.miti.gov.my

Ministry of Science, Technology, and the Environment (MOSTE).
www.mastic.gov.my/kstas/moste_f.htm

New Straits Times Press. www.nstpi.com.my

Sahabat Alam Malaysia: The A–Z of the Malaysian Environment.
http://surforever.com/sam/a2z/content2.html

The Star. www.thestar.com.my

The World Bank Group (type "Malaysia" in the search box). www.worldbank.org

The World-Wide Web Virtual Library: Malaysia. www.mtc.com.my/Virtual-Library/Malaysia.html

VIDEOS

Malaysia. Education 2000. Released 1996.

Video Visits: Mystical Malaysia—Land of Harmony. Ivn Entertainment. Released 1989.

BIBLIOGRAPHY

Bird, I. *The Golden Chersonese: Travels in Malaysia in 1879.* London: Oxford University Press, 1980.

Elder, Bruce. *Let's Go to Malaysia.* New York: Franklin Watts, 1984.

Major, John S. *The Land and People of Malaysia and Brunei.* New York: HarperCollins, 1991.

Malaysia in Pictures. Minneapolis: Lerner Publications, 1989.

Oshihara, Yuzuro. *Malaysia.* Milwaukee: G.Stevens Publishing, 1986.

Wright, David K. *Malaysia.* Chicago: Children's Press, 1988.

INDEX